MR. VESSEY OF ENGLAND

Being the Incidents and Reminiscences of Travel in a Twelve Weeks' Tour through the United States and Canada in the Year 1859

by John Henry Vessey

Edited by Brian Waters

(Introduction by
EARL SCHENCK MIERS)

In 1859 Mr. John Henry Vessey, an intelligent, likable young English gentleman, came to the United States as a tourist, and left us a portrait of our country and its people that has seldom been surpassed for candor, honesty, antipathy, and sympathy. In these pages we see ourselves of a hundred years ago as we appeared to an open-minded, inquiring visitor, and the picture is a fascinating one for us to read today. It is all the more interesting because Mr. Vessey, of course, had no idea of the approaching Civil War, nor, apparently, did the people he met. So here in these pages we stand, North and South, as we were seen and judged by this visitor.

He journeyed 11,000 miles "from the City of Quebec in the North to the cotton and rice fields of South Carolina, Georgia, and Alabama, in the South, to the prairies of the

(Continued on back flap)

(Continued from front flap)

West beyond the Mississippi, to the cities of Boston, New York, and Philadelphia in the East."

He recorded what he thought of cities and hotels, plantations and slave sales, Chicago (which he did not like) and Niagara Falls (which impressed him), and of the great variety of persons he encountered. "As a people I do not admire the Americans. They are such a conceited, self-sufficient, rough lot with the greatest love for their own country I ever met with, even more so than the Scotch. . . . At the same time, that self-reliance and go-aheadness has been the great secret of their unparalleled success as a people. In building cities, I consider they are far ahead of us. They are wanting in good roads. In hotels they are also far ahead of us." He was greatly interested in the problem of slavery, which he saw at its best and at its worst. He went to church and discussed politics and crops, and had his own highly individual opinions on everything.

The introduction by Earl Schenck Miers sets the times and background in proper perspective. This journal, edited by the writer's grandson, has never been published before, since Mr. Vessey of England was writing for himself alone.

Mr. Vessey of England

John Henry Vessey
(1827—1887)

MR. VESSEY
OF ENGLAND

—◦—◦—

*Being the Incidents and Reminiscences of
Travel in a Twelve Weeks' Tour through the
United States and Canada in the Year 1859*

BY JOHN HENRY VESSEY

Edited by Brian Waters

—◦—◦—

*G. P. Putnam's Sons
New York*

MANUFACTURED IN THE UNITED STATES OF AMERICA

VAN REES PRESS • NEW YORK

To the memory of his daughter Mary
with love from her son

INTRODUCTION

by Earl Schenck Miers

BY 1859, when John Henry Vessey arrived for a twelve-week tour of the United States and Canada, America had been jabbed so often by the pens of British visitors that the sight of another scribbling in his notebook must have evoked a kind of mute, sullen indifference. More than a quarter of a century had passed since the remarkable Mrs. Trollope had visited our shores and outraged our feelings with the publication of *Domestic Manners of the Americans*. We had learned by 1859 to look upon Mrs. Trollope with what we considered was a proper historical perspective (and which included, in hot-headed moments, dropping the final "e" from her name). At the time of Mrs. Trollope's visit, we reasoned, the Tories in England had been so hard-pressed to beat down democratic reform agitation in Parliament that Mrs. Trollope had been sent here to provide Tory propaganda by inventing libels about us. In our more dispassionate moods, we realized there never had been sufficient imagination among the Tories in

England to conceive of employing the acid wit of Mrs. Trollope in any such ingenious stratagem; for all that *Domestic Manners of the Americans* had been used with tremendous effectiveness in disparaging the democratic way of life, this result had been nothing more than sheer Tory luck.

Next to rankle American tempers was Charles Dickens, who, crossing the Atlantic (or, as Mr. Vessey would say, deciding "to put up with the horrors of seasickness"), came to judge for himself how well the noble experiment of democracy had functioned. In 1842 the appearance of *American Notes for General Circulation* revealed that Mr. Dickens had some real doubts about his American cousins. For example, traveling in the cabin of a river steamer, the famous novelist glanced down his nose and observed that "you might suppose the whole male portion of the company to be the melancholy ghosts of departed bookkeepers, who had fallen dead at the desk: such is their weary air of business and calculation." Doubtless every word of this criticism was justified; but the reasonable complaint that America had with Mr. Dickens, and with Mrs. Trollope (even granting her the dignity of that finale "e"), was the fact that there existed in the American character qualities both were incapable of understanding.

On both sides of the Atlantic we lived then in an altogether different emotional climate. The great social and political upheavals wrought by the Revolutionary War still stood on trial before the bar of history—most of all in

Britain, where the proposition that all men are created equal remained a source of unrest and change. In 1859, the year of Mr. Vessey's visit, the British intellect was especially sensitive to the social and philosophical pressures that were marching, along with the brick and mortar of the Industrial Revolution, into even the sanctuary of urban England; before that twelvemonth ended, both Charles Darwin's *The Origin of the Species* and John Stuart Mill's treatise *On Liberty* would be published. Then in another four years, upon the battlefield at Gettysburg, Lincoln defined what the American experiment was destined to demonstrate to the world—that a government of the people, by the people, and for the people could endure—and the impact of this victory would be great upon democratic movements in England and elsewhere.

Even before then, however, a noticeable change came into the attitude of the British visitor. The American habit of expectorating revolted him no less than it had Mrs. Trollope or Mr. Dickens, but his tone grew more moderate, his view broader, and within the limits of his opportunity and temperament he seemed to be exerting a conscious effort to be more objective and sympathetic. Mr. Vessey, our present chronicler, for all of his own deep Tory conviction, belonged to this newer pattern of British traveler, as did Anthony Trollope, who followed him to America in a very short time. Just what Mr. Vessey would have thought of us after the American experiment had withstood the bloody test of a civil war we can only conjecture;

at least it seems reasonable to suppose that he would not have disagreed entirely with Mr. Trollope's comment in 1873: "An Englishman visiting the United States ... should be ever guarding himself against the natural habit of looking at things only from his own point of view. . . . Should he find Americans to be educated, plenteously provided, honest, moral and Godfearing, he might perhaps, in such case, safely conclude that they were prosperous and happy, even if they talked through their noses and called him *Sir* at every turn in their speech. . . ."

Mr. Vessey did not pretend to be a literary man. As the modern traveler takes along his camera to record personal memories of his journey, so did Mr. Vessey arrive in New York with a thick octavo notebook, bound in morocco, on the cover of which the stationer had stamped in gold leaf *United States and Canada 1859*. Herein Mr. Vessey's quill pen set down the experiences he would like later to recall for his father and sisters, and whenever he stayed at a hotel with illustrated note paper he clipped off the letterhead and pasted it in his book. Eventually this volume found its way into the family bookcase, and now almost a hundred years later the public may have the pleasure of reading pages never intended for its scrutiny.

Candor is seldom without its charm, and so it proves with Mr. Vessey: his honesty limits his journal to what he sees and hears and experiences for himself. It is not difficult to find the Mr. Vessey of this journal an engaging companion, nor to share with him the irritations of train travel between

New York and Philadelphia, for his displeasures are not without modern parallels. He sees the City of Brotherly Love as "laid out in straight lines," which gives it, in a phrase, a becoming Quaker substance; a day in Baltimore is quite enough for one eager to observe slavery in the South; and his impressions of Washington are reasonably colored by the scandal that then rocked the capital—the trial of Daniel E. Sickles for the murder of Philip Barton Key (whose father had written "The Star-Spangled Banner"). An unfaithful wife, a political personage as defendant whose own indiscretions were notorious, a battery of defense lawyers led by the snappish Edwin M. Stanton all gave this occasion an atmosphere of judicial travesty. Mr. Vessey's opinions on the occasion were temperate compared to what he could have read, then and later, in the American press. Sassed the Baltimore *Patriot*, not entirely without cause: "We may somewhat account for the seeming tenderness and extreme delicacy of the prosecution on remembering the fact that the accused [Sickles] was a fast friend of the highest officer of the nation."

Of special interest to the student of life in ante-bellum America will be the account of Mr. Vessey's travels in the South. That he understood nothing of the impending conflict between the North and the secessionists was not unusual, for only a few perceptive Americans then did. The social hospitality of the South rarely extended to hospitality of the mind. The typical Southern planter knew where he stood on the question of the "peculiar institution," and he intended to fight to keep his system if the Black Republicans forced him to it, but the subject was one that he preferred not to discuss. Most of the time he didn't even read the bellicose outpourings of his own rabid spokesmen in the pages of the Richmond *Examiner* or *DeBow's Review*; he was simply dead set against the Northern meddlers, such as that old foghorn Greeley, and he kept his own quiet counsel, his mind made up. His customs, manners, and institutions he viewed as acts of Providence, fixed and final. They were not open to question. Accepted on these terms the amiability of the Southern planter could not be surpassed; he was far more at ease as a host than the Northerner and far more accustomed to respecting the amenities dictated by conventional politeness. Again, the shrewd Frederick Law Olmstead would describe a regional characteristic that surely would not have displeased Mr. Vessey: "The 'high-toned gentleman' (a Southern expression) ... is not an article of city manufacture, as the most cultivated people of the North are. He has a peculiar character, and peculiar habits—more like those of the 'old English gentleman' than any class to be found now, perhaps, even in England." It is not surprising that Mr. Vessey felt a warmth toward the South, and accepted it on its own terms.

Mr. Vessey, like the traveler in any age, is a historical witness rather than a historian, and what he largely perceives is impressions of facts rather than facts themselves. What later is called history often is a very quiet, a very elusive phenomenon—sometimes no more than a force growing in the mind of a leader who has not yet actually emerged (a role that Lincoln then occupied). At the time of Mr. Vessey's visit secession was a possibility partially accepted, both North and South; but the fact that secession also must mean war was not grasped by the great mass of Americans until after the firing on Sumter. Even then, the conflict developed into something that the architects of the Confederacy had been incapable of perceiving—into total war—and from that change stemmed ultimate tragedy for the Southern cause and salvation for the Union. Also we would learn from that experience that, in a republic, people build political systems to meet their environmental needs and fight wars to fit their political systems.

Thus, as we travel with Mr. Vessey through the South, what he observes comes to us in a new dimension. Then flood waters in Arkansas and lower Mississippi turn the journey northward—from Memphis to St. Louis, thence across the Illinois prairies to Chicago, Detroit and Canada. Indeed, everything has changed—the character of both land and people and, it almost seems, the livestock—and, considering the circumstance, we cannot but admire the mild good humor of his comments. Compared to the remarks of Mr. Dickens and Mr. Trollope under much the same circumstances, Mr. Vessey indeed keeps tongue in cheek with considerable pluckiness. He admires the miraculous growth and bustle of Chicago, for all that "the rakings of hell get out here"; and one regrets that unlike the Prince of Wales, who visited Chicago the following year, Mr. Vessey could not have enjoyed a few days of quail hunting on the nearby prairies along with such first-rate western spectacles as a prairie fire, a thunderstorm, and a flaming sunset.

By now we have grown to like Mr. Vessey very much; he is not a stiff-necked Englishman at all, but an unaffected gentleman who confesses his own prejudices and seems the more likable for them. When at last he returns home, we are only sorry that his visit wasn't longer, that he couldn't have seen more.

EARL SCHENCK MIERS

JOHN HENRY VESSEY
(1827–1887)

by Brian Waters

THE author of this book came to the United States not as an immigrant but as a tourist—a remarkable event in the year 1859, for John Henry Vessey was thirty-one, a bachelor and a farmer. There was, however, nothing of the potential American citizen about "Mr. Vessey of England" (as he is referred to in these pages), for he was heir to the fertile manor of Halton Holgate, a mile from the small town of Spilsby, in Lincolnshire.

His father, Samuel Vessey, had restored their ancient name from obscurity to affluence. For centuries his forebears had been yeomen, but the first Vessey to settle in Lincolnshire came as one of the Norman conquerors; their name is recorded among the forty signatures to Magna Carta.

There was nothing of the yeoman about Samuel Vessey; he farmed with his head and not by the sweat of his brow. His

15

breed of Lincoln Longwold sheep was renowned, and their rams populated the virgin sheepwalks of Australia and New Zealand. As a judge of man and beast, of land and stock, Samuel Vessey had the reputation of being the "cleverest man in Lincolnshire." It was part of Samuel's prescience that he should send his son to a great public school before it was famous. John Henry went to Uppingham (his name is one of the earliest on the school register), and after he left school at the age of seventeen he made his home with his father.

The relationship between a widower father and a bachelor son was a harmonious one, from which the younger man found independence from parental tutelage in foreign travel. He was an early holder of a British passport —Number 3469 (signed by the Foreign Secretary, Lord Clarendon), and with this he travelled across the plains of Hungary to Budapest before the first railway, a venture which showed considerable enterprise and originality of mind.

His experience as a traveller brought him to America. The heir to a baronetcy and an estate in Lincolnshire, Montgomery Massingberd, was lost in the United States, and Vessey was asked to find him. It was rather like looking for a needle in a haystack, and no mention of this mission occurs in his journal; but Vessey in his well-balanced way set out to enjoy the trip whatever the outcome. The zest with which he followed the trail is found in the pages of this book. He wrote with no idea of publication, but with a keenly observant mind, eagerly equipped to absorb everything he saw. A churchman and a Tory, he was opinionated, very English in his outlook, with that finer quality of being fair minded in recording his opinions, which are often tinged with his sense of humour. His eyes were wide open, and with his farming experience he did not have to be told twice about what he saw in the American countryside of a century ago.

Without being derivative his writing shares much of the quality of Arthur Young and William Cobbett, possessing the vivid touch for things that are to be seen no more. He unconsciously records the end of an epoch, before the cloud of Civil War was the size of a man's hand, and to one who was so favourably impressed by the South the conflict must have come as a shock. However, in that year Vessey married Elizabeth Wilkinson of Skryne Castle, Tara, and bought the manor of Welton le Wold in his native county, an estate of 1,139 acres on which he built the existing manor house. His four children, two sons and two daughters, were born here.

Despite the remoteness of his new home his life was busy and varied. He held twelve land agencies, among them that of the Corporation of the City of London, and was a Justice of the Peace for the Lindsey Division of Lincolnshire. After his father's death he continued to farm the Halton estate, as well as that of Welton, making the forty-mile journey between the two manors once a week in a gig. He farmed on a rotation of crops, and his last years were overshadowed by bad harvests and the agricultural depression of the 1880's. He died in 1887 at the age of sixty.

These notes are written by his only surviving grandson.

BRIAN WATERS

Mr. Vessey of England

IT is seldom that America is chosen as a tour by those fond of travelling and seeing the world, preferring rather to visit the cities of the old world than encounter the voyage across the Atlantic to witness the energy and enterprise of the people on the American continent in building cities and clearing forests.

It has always been a favourite project with me to see the boundless forests and prairies of the Far West, to visit the slave-holding states of the South, and form my own impressions of the people and their "peculiar domestic institution," as it is there called. But the great distance, the time necessary for such a journey, the horror of a voyage across the Atlantic, together with the great difficulty in finding an agreeable companion having the time at his disposal and the inclination to encounter such a journey, have hitherto prevented me carrying my project into effect. But finding the *Persia*, the favourite boat of the Cunard line of steamers, advertised to leave Liverpool for New York on the 19th of March, I went down to London (March 1st) to see her. On my arrival at Mr. Iver's office, I had great difficulty in getting permission to go on board, as she was undergoing her annual renovation, painting, etc. I was so pleased with all the arrangements and general cleanliness that I at once made up my mind to put up with the horrors of seasickness, and set off alone to see the Western World; consequently I took my Passage for the 19th March in Stateroom No. 26, Price £26.

March 14th: London. Made arrangements with the Union Bank to place a credit to my account with Messrs. Duncan and Sherman, Bankers, New York, and to take circular notes on their house in addition. Met with Mr. Urquhart at Woods Hotel, who very kindly invited me, when I visited Montreal, to call upon him.

March 15th: Did not go to Lincoln as I had intended, where I was summoned on a special jury, but returned to Halton to spend the day at home.

March 16th: Left home finally for York by the 11.20 train.

March 17th: Bought 49 Beasts at York and sent them home. Left York 3 P.M for Liverpool, Adelphi Hotel.

March 18th: Called upon Mr. Bourne, Claughton, Birkenhead, who very kindly gave me letters of introduction to his friend Mr. Brower, New York, and Mr. Neilson, Philadelphia. Called with him upon Messrs. Rogers and Calder. Mr. C gave me a letter of introduction to his brother in Charleston, South Carolina, and much information about the United States. Saw the Birkenhead Docks, Liverpool

Docks, warehouses, floating piers, etc., etc., and was altogether much pleased and greatly astonished at the magnitude of the shipping and the docks, which extend, I believe, upwards of five miles.

Called upon Mr. Graham, dined with him by appointment at his house, Rock Villa, New Brighton, where I met a very agreeable party, some of whom had been in the United States and many parts of South America. Mr. G gave me letters of introduction to his friends in New Orleans and strongly recommended me to visit Havana before I returned. Left at 9 with Mr. Graves to catch the Egremont boat, which we only just saved, and arrived at the Adelphi Hotel at 10 P.M. Wrote home.

March 19th: Adelphi Hotel, Liverpool. Up early to breakfast as the tugboat was advertised for 9 to take us to the *Persia.* There is a feeling in anticipation of a great event, which can be better imagined than described, which I must confess was my case this morning. In the coffee room I noticed many others like myself going by the *Persia* not enjoying their breakfast, some drinking wine, some one thing, some another, but few eating such a breakfast as they would have done had they not been commencing a sea voyage. Breakfast over and the cab at the door, I called at the Post Office for London letters on my way to the landing stage.

A steam tugboat (the *Satellite*) took us to the *Persia,* which was lying up the river about a mile. Despatched a newspaper home before leaving and set my watch Liverpool time to make the variation in time as we travelled westward. Set sail at 10 P.M, and at 11.30 passed the landing stage, took aboard the mails, fired two guns and bid adieu to old England.

The weekly postal communication between England and the United States (by the Cunard Line) greatly astonished me. I believe that more than fifty sacks of letters were brought on board that morning, to say nothing of newspapers which come down in a great van. The Liverpool wharfs, warehouses and shipping are seen to great advantage on passing down the river. Noticed Mr. Graham's house at New Brighton as we passed. It was a beautiful day and we kept the Welsh mountains in sight for many miles. Attended all meals on board and went to bed early. At 11 P.M. there was a cry: "A wreck, a wreck!" Those well enough ran on deck immediately to see what had happened. I was not among the number, but on emerging found that we had run down the brig *Agnes* bound for the West Indies with machinery on board. Although the shock was hardly perceptible to us on board the *Persia*, it struck her with such force that she quickly went down in ten minutes. It was with great difficulty that the hands, sixteen in number, were got on board the *Persia*. The time was so short. One man was missing.

On the following morning the *Canada* hove in sight, so we lowered the boats and put the people on board for Liverpool. It was a fearful sight to see these poor creatures, who had only just escaped with their lives. It created quite a gloom on board, but like railway accidents on land, such things are never talked about on board ship, as no doubt there was great neglect on the part of the watch. It was said that the cost to the company would be not less than £5,000.

March 20th: Sunday. Church of England service is read by the Captain (Judkins) in the saloon at half past ten on a Sunday morning. All the men and officers off duty attended and passengers who think fit to do so. After the prayer for the Queen and the Royal Family they read a similar one for the President of the United States (this is quite optional with the Captain, but is generally done to please the Yankee Passengers). I was too ill to stay the service over, so went below to my room and continued there all day.

March 21st: Monday. Rough, very ill.

March 22nd: Tuesday. Rather better.

March 23rd: Wednesday. Gradually better and got on deck and encountered the saloon at dinner. The great difficulty after seasickness is to sit in a saloon where others are eating. If you can once get over that you have made great progress towards convalescence.

March 24th: Thursday. Fine still morning, sea like a sheet of glass. The ocean has a most beautiful appearance when the sun is just rising, if there is no swell, which was the case this morning. It is a great mistake to call the waters blue, they are a clear green.

Two ships in sight, which is a novelty, as we have not seen a sail but our own since we lost sight of land. One day on board ship (when you are well) is so much like the last that there is little to describe. Time is divided into watches of four hours, every half hour the bell rings, at the hour two bells and so on till the eighth bell, which denotes the four hours watch when officers and men change duty. The watch between 4 and 8 P.M in fine weather is divided into two and called the Dog Watch. Riddle. Why is the watch between 4 and 8 called the Dog Watch? Because it is curtailed.

General routine on board:

Breakfast at 8.30
Luncheon   12.30
Dinner   4.0
Tea   8.0

Supper if you like till 10. Lights out in the saloon 11.30 P.M and in the bedrooms at 12.

March 25th: Friday, 4 P.M. Vessel in sight supposed to be in distress. Orders were immediately given for lowering No. 4 boat and to have everything in readiness, when we neared her as we quickly did as we were going fifteen or sixteen knots an hour. We found as we approached her that instead of being waterlogged as the Captain thought she was, it was merely a French fishing boat, which having lost her bearings wished to know from us in what Lat. and Long. she lay. We looked very like being *sold,* and our Captain was not in very capital humour the remainder of that day, which I don't wonder at, as the stopping of a powerful steamer like the *Persia* loses some time that they can ill

26

afford, considering the great competition they have to encounter.

At 12 each day they take the time, if the weather is clear and they can get an observation; if not they ascertain by dead reckoning as they throw out the line every two hours, which denotes the number of knots an hour the vessel is running. Variations in time today 2 hours 58 minutes from Liverpool (London time).

March 26th: Saturday. Variation in time 3.17. Very cold, which denotes that we are in the neighbourhood of ice. At 5 P.M. saw a floating iceberg in the distance. As the *Canada* had reported much ice we worked to the southwards, which accounted for us seeing so little.

March 27th: Sunday. Prayers as usual in the saloon at 10.30. The old shepherd, as we called him (one of the passengers), was rather sold, having spent a week preparing a sermon. The Captain asked another minister to preach, who not expecting it was quite unprepared; it created no little amusement. Variation in time 3.49.

March 28th: Monday. Variation in time 4.7. Dense fog and very cold.

March 29th: Tuesday. Variation in time 4.37. Dense fog and great swell. Anticipating seeing land at daybreak we were in great spirits, for there is great monotony in nothing but sky and water for so many days. Drank the Captain's health and made a collection for the band. (£10.6s among forty saloon passengers)

March 30th: Wednesday. Land in sight at daybreak and

the pilot on board. What a glorious sight it is to have land in view; only to be really appreciated by those who have been on the ocean for some days. It is wonderful how different your fellow passengers look when they near land and doff their sea caps, and appear in black hats (a thing unknown at sea). The harbour of New York strikes a stranger as a most easy place to protect, the entrance being very narrow; a fortress on each side would be very difficult to pass. Although it is a magnificent bay, the appearance is not so imposing as you enter by water, as seen from the Battery, where you obtain a grand view of it. Manhattan Island on which stands New York is divided from Brooklyn by the East River, and from New Jersey city by the North or Hudson River.

I was surprised to find the foliage so backward on entering the harbour, after leaving the trees and hedges in England nearly in leaf. Met the *Asia* in the harbour ready to leave for England at 12. Very fortunate to arrive in time to send letters by her. Fired two guns to announce our arrival, and at 10.30 A.M left the *Persia* by steam tug to the New Jersey Ferry where our baggage is examined by the Custom House Officers. Very little trouble with them. Surprised on leaving the *Persia* to find what a slight mark the collision with the *Agnes* had made upon her.

Took a carriage with Biddu, Kennard and others and made our way to the St. Nicholas Hotel, Broadway, New York. The public carriages in America belonging to the hotels are built in a most peculiar style, having more the appearance of an old discarded Lord Mayor's Coach than anything else; holding nine people inside, others at the top with baggage packed on behind. You cross the Hudson River from New Jersey to the New York side by a ferry boat, which like the stages are peculiar to this country. They drive the carriage direct onto the boat, and when they have got on board as many as the boat will hold, away they steam to the other side, and you drive onto the shore as soon as the boat stops. In fact the passengers in the carriages need not know that they are crossing the water at all. The fare for foot passengers is one cent.

New York. Thanks to a protecting Providence here we are safely landed on the shores of the Western World after a most favourable voyage of eleven days from England.

Arrived at the St. Nicholas Hotel about 12; exceedingly glad to get on land and change our sea clothes and have a bath. After luncheon sallied forth into Broadway to "form an impression" (as the Yankees say) of the great city.

New York has not exactly that foreign look which strikes a stranger on first landing on the continent of Europe, still there is a strangeness in everything you see around you. The style of buildings with their Venetian shutters, carriages, dress and appearance of the people all combine to impress you with the conviction that you are not in the old country, notwithstanding every man you meet speaks the English language.

The St. Nicholas Hotel is on a scale of magnificence un-equalled by anything of the kind I have ever witnessed in

Europe. It is the greatest hotel in Christendom in the hotel-keeping line, accommodating upwards of a thousand guests when full. The general managements of the hotel are very good. Magnificent dining saloons, drawing rooms to which you can retire if you think fit, or if you are a smoker the bar is a convenient lounge; very different to the bar of an inn in England. It is an immense room fitted up entirely for smoking, the floor paved with black-and-white Marble. At one end are sold cigars, opera tickets etc., etc., at the other the drinks common with the Americans such as Brandy Smash, Mint Julep, Gin Slings etc., etc. Adjoining this room is the billiards room containing ten tables, which appeared to me to be fully employed excepting Sundays. Further on are news rooms where you can see the news I may say of the world; whether you want to know what is going on at St. Petersburg, Paris or London, or if you wish to know the latest price of niggers in the New Orleans Markets, it is all posted up there.

The barber's shop is an indispensable luxury of an American hotel. You generally find one on the first floor, near to the bar, and the business carried on there is only second to the billiards tables. The room is never empty. I believe that at the St. Nicholas eight men are constantly employed in this department and each man is supposed to earn six dollars a day. The beds are very good. There is a uniform charge at these monster hotels, you pay 2 Dol. and a half a day, which includes everything but wine. You can eat at any hour of the day you please from 5 A.M to 12 at night and everything is provided on the most liberal scale.

Considering the number of guests at these hotels there is less bustle and confusion than a stranger would suppose. An Englishman would think that the ringing of bells in a house of this magnitude somewhat alarming, but you never hear a bell ring in the hotels of the United States. When you pull the bell in your room it strikes an indicator down in the office, denoting what number it is. It is one man's business to attend to that indicator (together with all letters, parcels and keys of bedrooms). The moment a number is struck he immediately beckons a waiter and sends him to your room, putting the number back in its place. The great advantage of which is that if twenty bells rang at the same time he would know which were unanswered by the numbers remaining out. I wonder the plan is not adopted in the English hotels. Two other men are always in attendance in the bar, receiving money, giving directions what rooms you are to have and general routine of the hotel. Another man is baggage master, attending to the baggage on the arrival and departure of every train. It is very amusing to sit in the entrance hall or bar of one of these hotels and see the tide of people, representing all parts of the United States, constantly moving: one man perhaps ordering his baggage for New Orleans, another St. Louis and so on. The whole available space is generally filled with men smoking, spitting and chewing all day long, come in when you will. They are the most disgusting set of people I ever came across. Chewing and spitting is carried on to such an extent and with such *precision* that a Yankee one day in the cars had to spit some distance out of the window, very much to the annoyance of a lady near him. He coolly observed, "Don't be alarmed, ma'am, I am a very good shot."

All the best hotels have a separate entrance for ladies, which is very necessary for their comfort, as the principal entrance would be anything but pleasant for a lady to pass, crowded as it generally is with such smoking, spitting, tobacco-chewing Yankees.

Called upon Mr. Brower 45 South St., from home. Also upon Messrs. Cutler and Levitt, who have a large connection in the Southern States. Very kindly gave me many letters through Georgia, Alabama, etc. Dined at the five o'clock Table d'Hote with Mr. Dobell, and in the evening went with him to Laura Kerne's Theatre to see *Our American Cousin.* The acting I thought good of its kind. The English nobleman is a perfect burlesque, but it takes with the Yankees. Called at the Metropolitan Hotel to see "Old Missouri," as we called him, one of our passengers in the *Persia.* The American theatres are not fitted up in that style you see in the best London houses, but the charge is low in proportion.

March 31st: Thursday. Called upon Capt. Judkins at the Everett House, Union Square, who accompanied me to Messrs. Cunard, where I secured a berth in the *Persia,* No. 43, 44 for the return voyage 25th May, knowing the difficulty there is at that season in procuring one in a favourite ship like the *Persia*. Took the entire berth, paying 1½ fare, equal to £39 English money, rather than run the risk of a Yankee for a companion, well knowing their filthy habits.

Presented my letters to Messrs. Duncan and Sherman, Bankers, and made necessary monetary arrangements with them for obtaining through their agents what money I might require through the States. I would recommend anyone taking a similar tour, which I should do myself, if I ever travel through that country again, not to deposit any money with an American firm, but take circular notes on a London bank, as the rate of exchange is generally against you, and on the circular notes you only lose on the amount you draw. Mr. Duncan, having just returned from Cuba, gave me much information about the South. Hotels, etc., and also letters to friends of his in New Orleans. Agreeably surprised to find a portrait of Sir Peter Laurie * in Mr. Duncan's room at the bank, which reminded me very much of home.

April 1st: Called upon Mr. Brower, 45 South St., who was most kind. He gave me and obtained through his friends many very valuable introductions in the South, also much information about the growth of cotton. His friends live principally in Texas, but being so intimately connected with cotton himself, and taking such a great interest in the slavery question, he expresses himself particularly anxious that

---

* A Lord Mayor of London and a friend of the Vesseys.—Ed.

33

I should see slavery in the South, as it is, and judge for myself, and not act as so many of our countrymen do in visiting America. That is to travel through the Northern States, where neither rice nor cotton are grown, then down to New Orleans as an atonement for what they have missed in the South. I have met with men in my short experience who certainly have been to America and are ready to discuss the slavery question, but whose travels probably never took them into the slave states. Consequently they know as little of the actual relative position of slave and slave holder as though they had never left New York. He hoped if my travels brought me back by way of New York I should not fail to give him my opinions from what I had seen of plantation life.

Having now obtained *my credentials for the South,* and knowing that the climate would be warm enough by the time I arrived at Charleston, I thought it better to see New York on my return, and therefore lost no time in proceeding South.

Broadway rather disappointed me, having heard so much of it. It is certainly a very fine street, but not nearly so wide as the name would lead you to suppose. Although it contains many magnificent marble stores, such as Stewarts, and hotels like the St. Nicholas, all of white marble, there is a great want of uniformity, many of those stupendous blocks of buildings joining houses of very inferior description. The streets radiating from Broadway are the filthiest I ever saw, with mud nine inches deep, more like a ploughed field in wet weather, having been carted over, than a town street. This is among the *advantages* of a pure democracy. Men who have risen to wealth quickly get the control of the municipal government (used to dirt and mud in their early days) and don't see the necessity of cleansing the streets.

The pavements on those streets (such as Wall St., Pine St., etc.) are a foot higher than the road, which is a very necessary precaution for foot passengers, as the draymen are not at all particular how they drive. The police regulations must be bad. You see drays backed up upon the foot pavements to the warehouses, foot passengers having to take care of themselves, for Jarvey is not any respecter of persons in this country. On the contrary people of that class here have a great pleasure in asserting the *equality* of mankind. The style of buildings in these side streets is good, which shows the great contrast between these people and our own country. Their buildings are good, notwithstanding the dirty streets by which they are surrounded. What a fearful dust there must be when this dries up! It is even more striking in Western cities, where the buildings are of a very superior order with streets unpaved. Omnibuses are the principal means of conveyance through the main streets. No one thinks of taking a cab in New York. Their fares are so exceedingly high, and you have to put up with an amount of incivility from the driver unequalled in any city in Europe. The best and only way is to keep to the public conveyances, particularly if you have any knowledge of the place, as five cents is the fare, whether you go twenty yards or the entire length of Broadway, which you pay on entering. There is no conductor, but the driver has a small hole in the side through which he puts his hand for the money, and a little box near him, holding any small change. They are very sharp not to lose a fare. In many streets railway-omnibuses run, pulled by two mules, which are very convenient and run easily. I one day wanted a cab from Union Square to the St. Nicholas, which is not more than half a mile, and asked Cabby "How much?" 1½ Dol., 6s 3d. English. I told Jarvey if he took us for greenhorns he must let us go, as we had both been from home before. After offering to take us for the *moderate fare of one dollar*, he was most abusive because we preferred taking the street railway at five cents. They are the most independent set of fellows I ever came across. Only those who have had any dealings with the New York Jarvey can realise the idea of the anecdote they tell of a foreign prince visiting the country, and ordering a carriage. After waiting at the door of the hotel some time, up drives Jarvey and says, "Are you the chap that ordered this carriage, as I guess that I am the gent that is going to drive you."

You seldom see a coachman in livery unless he be a black man. White bear and buffalo skins are usually worn as carriage aprons and look remarkably well. The horses have not that sleek, glossy skin you see in London. I suppose the winters are so cold they dare not keep the hair so close;

therefore at this season of the year they look as though they had wintered at grass, and only been up a week or two.

Their carriages are peculiarly light and easy to run. The wheels must be made of the best material to stand the wear and tear of the streets, considering that the spokes are not more than a third of the thickness of those in English carriages. The American light buggy wagon for one or a pair of horses, without the top, weighs from 175 to 220 lbs. They generally drive their horses either without bluffs, or with much smaller ones than we use. Their horses are admirably trained. They must have a better method than we have for you seldom see a restive horse. Oftener you see one left in the streets or tied to a post, but perfectly quiet. They never use a whip to drive. The more you pull an American horse the faster he goes, only say "Whoa" and he will stop in a moment. Riding is not the fashionable amusement with the American people, they all seem to delight in driving these fast trotting horses in the light buggys. Their racing is all in this style; 2 minutes 40 seconds used to be their maximum speed, but I believe during my stay in the country, one horse trotted the mile in 2 minutes 24½ seconds.

April 1st cont: Met Mr. Dobell (Quebec) at 11 by appointment at 87 Beaver St., who, at the invitation of his friend Mr. —, took us to see the naval dockyard at Brooklyn. There is but little for an Englishman to see in an American dockyard, after seeing Portsmouth and Plymouth in the old country. After parting with my friend Mr. Dobell, who had to leave that afternoon for St. John's, New Brunswick, I spent the remainder of the day in seeing the great lions of the city, not forgetting Fifth Avenue, which is the Belgravia of New York, comprising the best residences in the city. At the upper end of this street is the Croton Reservoir by which the city is supplied with water, which is brought a distance of forty miles. It is considered a grand piece of engineering, as the water is carried by an aqueduct across the Harlem river for a considerable distance.

I have elsewhere mentioned the dinner card of the St. Nicholas Hotel, the one below is the breakfast card, which together show that a man need not starve in these Monster Hotels, and anyone who finds fault with the living in this hotel I would class with the style of man you sometimes meet with finding fault with the waiters. I always take that man to have but few servants at home.

April 2nd: Left New York at 8 A.M for Philadelphia. The railway cars are built on a very different construction to those on our English lines. They are a great length, holding from fifty to sixty people with a road down the centre, and doors at each end. The seat on each side holds two and is reversible. They are very similar in accommodation and speed to the second class on the Lombard Venetian lines between Milan and Venice.

The American trains do not run so fast as the English, neither would it be safe, as their roads are not so permanently constructed. The fares are from three to four cents a mile, one class for all (excepting niggers, who have a carriage to themselves), so the President of the Great Republic or any of its unwashed sons may sit side by side in the cars on the most perfect equality.

On a long journey it is desirable to take a through ticket, as you have always the privilege of *laying over*, as they call it. If you wish to remain anywhere on the way, and resume your journey on the following or any future day, your ticket is still available by merely getting it counterstamped by the conductor, whenever you take the cars again. It is a great convenience in their long distances, but such a thing in England would create great confusion where our journeys are so short. Although their fares appear low, their accommodation is on a par with it. Some things in connection with their system of Railroad (they never say Railway in this country) travelling might be advantageously adopted on our English lines, for instance the checking of baggage. When your baggage arrives at the station, the baggage master enquires your destination. He then gives you a duplicate number of the one he attaches to each piece of baggage you have, and on arrival you merely have to state the hotel where you stay, and give up that ticket or tickets, when you may rely upon everything being in the room of your hotel, without any further trouble, beyond the payment of one shilling (¼ Dol.). The omnibus fare to the hotel is the same.

At the top of the carriage is a cord running the entire length of the train, communicating with the driver, by which means if anything be wrong he can be apprised of it in a moment from any part of the train: instead of the bell being in the station (as in England), the driver has a bell on the engine, which he rings previous to starting. He and the stoker are protected from the weather by a little framework of glass.

At minor stations in England, instead of the expensive waiting rooms and platforms, how much might have been saved by carriages constructed on the American plan; that is, a projection at the end with steps on each side down to the ground. Such innovations might be thought very democratic in the old country; but if adopted in the first instance, what an enormous expense might have been saved.

Although some of their plans are improvements on ours, I cannot for a moment compare their system with our own. Their lines are badly constructed, and often not fenced, and many of their bridges, culverts, etc., are made in a very temporary manner, chiefly of wood, as the fearful accidents amply prove. Everything must be done quick in this country, often without the slightest regard to safety.

As soon as the train leaves the station, the Conductor walks through the cars to issue tickets to any fresh passengers who have not got them, as it is not necessary to take your ticket at the station before getting into the carriage. He then, after having inspected your ticket, gives you a small pink card of the line, giving on one side the various stations and distances from each other, and on the other side the following notice: "Stick this check in your—" (the blank being filled with the little figure of a hat). It was too

Yankee a notion for me to put up with, so I always put mine in my pocket, and if the conductor demanded it, I always showed it until he was tired of asking. But I must say with all their democracy and pride of equality they always show respect to an Englishman.

After you have got fairly started, and the conductor has satisfied himself that everyone has paid, for they are "mighty cute" not to miss anyone, in comes a boy selling newspapers, books and periodicals. When he has tired the passengers with literature, he then brings oranges, nuts and apples. After a time he will bring sweetmeats, chinese puzzles, etc., any dodge to raise a cent.

I find that they get fifteen cents in the Dol. for what they sell, others give a dollar a day for the privilege and make what they can, you may judge they are "pretty smart" (a Yankee phrase) in vending their wares. Smart in this country means quick, clever. To speak of a clever man they mean a goodtempered, amiable man. Elegant is a great word with them. We call all Americans Yankee, a Yankee is properly a native of the New England States, a thorough down-Easter from near the sun rising.

Iced water is always at hand at the end of every carriage with a small drinking cup attached, if not a boy hands water round to the passengers at intervals. Although with us such a thing may seem unnecessary, it is quite the reverse here, among these disgusting tobacco-chewing Yankees. I believe they would go mad if it were not for the plentiful supply of water in the cars to such an extent is it carried. No one but those who have travelled in the States can have any idea of the disagreeable feeling there is when you enter the cars in a morning. The smoking room of an inn in the morning is nothing to it.

The fields are sometimes fenced from the line but not always. The road crossings are merely marked by a notice board in large letters BEWARE OF THE LOCOMOTIVE. In England they would be constantly running over children, and accidents continually happening in the environs of large towns, but here the trains run by houses totally unprotected from the line, for as Murray says, "It would be as easy to run over a cock sparrow as a Yankee boy."

I was much surprised to find so many stumps of trees, and land in such an unenclosed state between two such cities as New York and Philadelphia, but the land is poor in quality, and I find the settlers go West in preference to cultivating the old cleared land well. The stumps stand out of the ground two or three feet, and remain many years, if they are pine or hard wood, in fact the land they call cleared stands thicker with stumps than a well-planted orchard in England would be.

The land has a poor, sterile look. The wheats are looking well, which is all the corn we see up, as it is too early for the Indian corn. In many places the straw of last year's crop is still standing where it grew. The land appears to be so totally lost for want of drainage that you never see an entire plot of wheat looking well. The lower parts are generally swamp, I suppose labour is too high and land not of sufficient value to drain. There are no hedges. The white thorn will not grow in America. The fields are enclosed with post and rail, or more general is the snake fence.

We cross much water, and at one place leave the cars, cross over in boats and take other cars to Philadelphia, where we arrived about 12.

Girard House: Recommended to me as the best, if it is so I am sorry Philadelphia does not supply a better inn. The exterior is very good, but it is sadly wanting in cleanliness and light, very important considerations in the selection of a comfortable hotel.

Philadelphia is laid out in straight lines, crossed at right angles, which causes a wonderful sameness in the streets. Those running north and south are named after trees, as Chestnut, Pine, Walnut, Spruce, etc. The cross streets are numbered; it is the easiest place possible for a stranger to find his way, if you have occasion to ask, which is not often. The peculiarity of the answer struck me; a Yankee would say, "Eight blocks 39th and Chestnut," meaning that the street was eight blocks (i.e. squares of buildings) off, where 39th Street crosses Chestnut Street, and he would probably be half way down the street before you had time to ask another question. You never get a Yankee to use more words over such an occasion than are absolutely necessary to explain his meaning, he is always in such a fearful hurry. The houses in Philadelphia are particularly well built of red brick, and have a very clean and neat appearance, the basements are usually of white marble four or five feet

43

high. The doors and windows are all white, the pavements red brick, and one street so much like another that the place reminds you of a woman's twin babies.

The Quakers, I believe, are a very numerous body here. The appearance of the place would strengthen you in that opinion as it is the most prim place I ever saw.

Chestnut Street is the best and contains the leading shops.

Called upon Mr. Neilson, 1301 Spruce St., from whom I received every kindness, and very valuable information. I found him a most intelligent man, and particularly well informed on the subject of slavery, having lived in the West Indies twenty-four years. Being well acquainted with a hot climate he gave me many suggestions which I found very useful when I got into the South. Philadelphia is a great place for churches. All religious denominations here are on an equal footing, so every place of worship is called a church.

The Girard College is the most prominent public institution in the city. The founder, Stephen Girard, commenced life as many before him have done with a clear head and steady perseverance. In early life he went to sea, and afterwards settled in Philadelphia as a merchant, where he became one of the leading men of the place. He died at a great age, having amassed a great fortune (£1,500,000) and leaving no children, nor anyone to whom he cared to bestow his great wealth (excepting £28,000, which he left to his poor relations), he bequeathed the residue of his fortune in the hands of Trustees for the building and endowment of this college which bears his name. It is founded for the maintenance and education of poor orphan boys of the City of Philadelphia, who from the time of their entrance (five to sixteen years of age) are sufficiently provided for, and afterwards apprenticed to some trade or profession.

In Mr. Girard's will is the following reservation, which I think showed his great knowledge of human nature, and it would be well if the same proviso were made in many similar public institutions in the old country.

> I enjoin and require that no ecclesiastic missionary or minister of any sect whatever shall ever hold any station or duty whatever in the said college.
>
> In making this restriction I do not mean to cast any reflection upon any sect or person whatsoever, but as there are such a multitude of sects, and such a diversity of opinion amongst them, I desire to keep the tender minds of the orphans, who are to receive advantage from this bequest, free from the excitement which clashing doctrines of sectarian controversy are apt to produce.

There are something more than three hundred orphans in the College at the present time. There are many other public buildings in the city, among which are the Custom House and the United States Mint, but they contain but little interest to the passing visitor.

Philadelphia is well supplied with water from a reservoir at Fairmont, a distance of three or four miles out of the city; will amply repay a visit, not from any engineering skill displayed, but merely to show by what a simple and inexpensive process such a large city can be supplied with water. The river is held up perhaps half a mile back, which gives a sufficient elevation to the water that turns six powerful waterwheels, continually at work throwing the water up into the reservoir.

April 3: Sunday. Spent the day with Mr. Neilson and went to the Episcopal Church. Philadelphia is a wonderful place for free blacks, and Sunday is a great day for them. They are fond of great contrasts, for you generally see them dressed with as much white as possible.

Mr. N. has the most thorough contempt for the Yankee character of any man I ever met. I was much surprised when he told me his age as we parted. He is a fine old man, very intelligent, one of the old sterling sort fast dying out. I was sorry to say goodbye as we shall probably never meet again. He gave me much information about the growth of cotton and slavery, and recommended me to obtain if possible Patent Office reports on agriculture when I got to Washington.

April 4th: Monday. Left Philadelphia at 8 A.M. for Baltimore, where we arrived at 1 P.M. Stayed at Gilmour's Hotel, for Mr. Duncan in his list of hotels gave me two at each place, one as the Monster Babel Hotel, and the other a quieter house, but where I should not see so much American life. I was so disgusted with the Girard House at Philadelphia that I thought I would try the other style. I was pleased I did so.

Baltimore, a clean, well-built city, gives you the idea of a "well-to-do" place. Beyond a marble statue to Washington from the top of which you can form a good estimate of the town, and a smaller statue in the square opposite the hotel, there is nothing of peculiar interest to a stranger. A drive after dinner round the place is all that is required to see Baltimore. During dinner I heard some Americans discussing English character, and speaking of some of their friends, who had been to *Eu rope*, as they call it. They observed among other peculiarities of the Britishers that they are so affected in their manners, so different from us (Americans). It struck me, "What a contemptible lot are these people to discuss manners." Men who are either picking their teeth after dinner or chewing tobacco with the accompaniments. Women laughing and talking in the most vulgar manner.

April 5th: Left Baltimore 8.50 for Washington (thirty-eight miles). Willards Hotel good. Met a better class of Americans here than I have seen since I came into the country. The general character of the country is flat, but as we approach Washington it becomes more undulating though poor land. I have been much struck with the poverty of the soil, which is of a poor yellow loam or sand, expecting to see a fine, black alluvial soil, but they tell you here you must go Westwards to see that.

After the Capitol, the Patent Office is the most imposing public building in Washington; built of white marble, it is the public register office, containing a model of every patent

47

granted in the United States, and many other works of interest; in fact a general museum. Obtained here Patent Office Reports for 1857 on Agriculture which are an Annual Register of the progress in that department throughout the States; also very valuable information respecting the growth of cotton, as to what lands are most suitable for that purpose, what portion is in timber, open plains, or prairies.

1856 Report contains in answer to Government enquiry replies from their consuls in various parts of the world, whether cotton can be advantageously grown in their respective localities compared with the Southern States of America.

Opposite to the Patent Office is the Post Office, a very fine building, and at the upper end of the same street are the Treasury Offices. All the public offices here being built of white marble have a very ornamental appearance.

The President's house stands at the back of the Treasury fronting the other way. It is nothing more than a plain stone-built house, just fit for a country gentleman's residence. I was much surprised as it is not a house suitable for a man holding such an important position in the country. A stranger would sooner take the Patent Office as the Residence of the President of the Great Republic. A gentleman at Willards asked me if I should call upon the President. I said, "Certainly not," as I had no introduction to him. He said, "Never mind about that, if you go you will find him very glad to see you as an Englishman." I found that he gave audiences about 2 o'clock, and as that gentleman told me it was not considered an intrusion on the part of a stranger like myself to pay respects to him, I therefore presented myself at the White House at the appointed hour. I was ushered up into the reception room, where I found others on the same errand, but to my surprise instead of making a formal bow and passing on he entered into conversation with some of them. When my turn came I apologised to him for presenting myself without an introduction, but that I was an Englishman, travelling through the United States on pleasure, and had taken the liberty of calling upon him. I found him very affable and courteous, he shook me by the hand and wished me to sit down (much to my surprise as I have observed before).

He said "I am glad to see you. It is the custom and privilege of this great country for the highest and lowest to meet together with the utmost freedom." After a short conversation about the country, the Capitol, and what I thought of the great city of New York (an American never fails in speaking of his own country to ask that question. I believe that many of them have an impression that it is a larger city than London), but of course it was not so with the President (Buchanan), as he had resided in London many years, and asked me many things about the great city. After making my formal bow, I retired and was much gratified that I had taken my friend's advice, and only regretted that I had not some English friends with me to have a good joke over the matter.

Went to the Capitol, which is a magnificent building of

white marble, comprising both Houses of Parliament. It stands in a most commanding position in grounds of considerable extent, laid out in gardens and pleasure grounds, being built at one end of the Pennsylvania Avenue, the Treasury Offices being at the other.

It struck me what a pity our Houses of Parliament are not in an equally good position in one of our parks. From the top of the Capitol you obtain perhaps the best view of the city and surrounding country. Met with great civility from a man I accidentally fell in with in going over the Senate House, who showed me over the whole place, and very kindly procured me a copy of the Patent Office Report 1856, which I was anxious to obtain, containing as it does much information about the growth of cotton. The more so as they are not to be bought, a limited number only being published annually for distribution among the senators and their friends, and being Government reports no doubt are based upon information on which you may rely. Bought some views of the place, and went to the Post Office, as we had telegraphed news of the arrival of the European Mail. No letters, so gave directions to forward them to Charleston. Wrote home, also to J. Woolley and requested him to answer me in Montreal, as a letter takes about five or six weeks before you get a reply.

The trial of Sickles for shooting Key is exciting much interest here. It commenced on Monday the 4th inst., but for the last two days they have been unable to form a jury of unbiassed men. Such is the go-ahead character of these people that they try a man by public opinion beforehand and when they are summoned on a jury to try him on *the evidence* they swear they are not unbiassed, having expressed an opinion. Such indeed has been the case for the last three days that they have summoned about seventy men each day, and only got three or four to stand on the jury. What a state of things in this free and enlightened republic. I wish that some Englishmen sighing at home for more liberty than would do them good would come out here, and see how democratic institutions work in this country. They would probably return more satisfied with our own form of Government.

The soil of this country is certainly not genial to the tree of liberty.

Since writing these notes on the spot, the Sickles trial is over, resulting in his acquittal (American morality versus English). The Americans are perfectly satisfied with the verdict, considering him quite justified in shooting Key. The English and Canadians on the other hand would have brought in a verdict of manslaughter.

April 7th: Left Washington 6.30 A.M. for Richmond, Va. (four hours). We then proceed by steamboat on the Aguia Creek for some miles, then take the cars for Richmond. We breakfast on board and pass through some very pretty scenery on each side of the river. A few miles from Washington is Mount Vernon, the burial place of Washington, their great patriot for whose memory they show the greatest respect. A small bell tolls as we pass the spot, when all Yankees take off hats, which is generally during breakfast. I don't think that any true-born American would dare to go through the operation of breakfasting during the ringing of that bell. I was quite amused to think they should make so much fuss of it, we English went on with our meal as usual. We arrived in Richmond a little after 2 and found dinner going on at Ballards Hotel, which was very acceptable after our early breakfast at Washington, for the meal on board those steamboats is only a matter of form. I always made it a point, whenever any public meal was going on, to sit down and join them, whether it was the proper time of day or not, which rule will generally hold good in travelling. Here we have slaves in abundance, this is the first place I have seen them in large numbers. The waiters in the hotel are all slaves.

Richmond, the capital of the state of Virginia, is pleasantly situated on high ground with good water communication (which latter observation applies to all American towns), and has a older look than many American cities I have yet seen. The Capitol (Court House) stands in a prominent position, and within the grounds is a statue of Washington. It is a pleasant drive round the town, which is all that is required to see. The streets are well laid out on the American plan with no material on the roads as usual. Trees are planted on each side of the street, which gives the town a very ornamental appearance. They are now in leaf (April 7th) and the fruit trees in full blossom. We are getting perceptibly warmer than New York.

The train today ran through a drove of cows and killed one of them. We hardly felt the shock in the cars, they are so long. We pulled up a few minutes to get the dead body off the line. They seemed to take it very quietly. I suppose such accidents often occur. The only wonder is they are not more frequent, as the lines are seldom fenced.

One of our passengers had two little boys with him (blacks), twelve or thirteen years of age, which he had just purchased at six hundred dollars each, and was taking them down South. He seemed particularly careful over them, and I wondered that he should show such anxiety over these boys, not for a moment thinking that they were slaves. Piccolomini is to sing here tonight. The beasts we see in passing along through this part of the country are small, not unlike Irish, but of a bad sort. It struck me that a cross with our shorthorns would be beneficial, but they must retain their hardiness to a certain extent as they have to live in the woods. It appears to me whenever a piece of land becomes cleared they keep it for arable, and run their cows and hogs in the woods, where they have an unlimited stray. Mules are worked chiefly in the drays, but that observation applies the more you get South, I suppose they stand the climate better and are more hardy.

Virginia being the state where tobacco is chiefly raised, I made many enquiries respecting its growth. It was not the season of the year to see it growing, but from information I obtained I find the seed is sown in beds on some rich alluvial soil in January. The land is then prepared, and the plants set in May or the beginning of June, in rows three feet by three feet, three inches apart. (The word planter more properly applies to the tobacco planter than to the man who raises cotton and rice which are both sown.)

The tobacco is topped in July and August, eight leaves are allowed to grow on each stem, or if the soil be very rich ten or twelve leaves. All suckers are broken off continually. The Green Worm and Tobacco Fly are its great enemies. It is ready to cut at the end of September; five plants to the pound is a good crop. It is considered an extra good one where four plants produce a pound. Value, ten dollars per hundred pounds. Land on which it is grown worth twenty-five dollars per acre, but with Guano it may be grown on inferior land, worth not more than five dollars per acre, cultivated by slave labour.

The above information is from a Virginian planter I met on the banks of the Mississippi. I can't look upon these Virginian and Maryland slave holders with the same forebearance as I can the cotton planters of the South, where the climate demands African labour. Here it is not so. They can cultivate their tobacco by free labour if required, but the natural increase of slaves are drafted off and sold down in the Southern markets, as we should raise young horses for sale in England.

Negroes for sale. I have just received ONE HUNDRED LIKELY NEGROES from Virginia and Maryland, among them some good Blacksmiths, Cooks, Washers and Ironers, all of which are for sale on accommodating terms for cash or good city acceptance, and I will be receiving fresh lots during the season. Those intending to purchase would do well to call at my office, corner Chartres and Esplanade streets, opposite the house of John B. Smith

Joseph Bruin

JUST ARRIVED, WITH A CHOICE LOT OF VIRGINIA NEGROES, consisting of Plantation Hands, Blacksmiths, Carpenters and House Servants and will be receiving fresh supplies during the season of the best Negroes that can be bought in the Virginia and Carolina markets, which I offer for sale on the most reasonable terms, cash or approved paper.

Office corner of Esplanade and Chartres streets, New Orleans.

John B. Smith

FOSTERS SLAVE DEPOT—The undersigned most respectfully presents this his card to the public at large for the coming season, in the sale of Slaves. Shall have constantly on hand a large and carefully selected stock of Slaves, calculated to please the purchaser, let his wants be what they may. Having three extensive yards, I am prepared to accommodate *five hundred slaves*. I also have every accommodation for traders, both for boarding and lodging with servants in attendance. My business will be solely confined to a commission, giving thereby each and every trader an equal opportunity in the disposal of his Negroes. Thankful for past favours, I respectfully solicit a continuance of all former customers and friends.

April 8th: Left Richmond 5 A.M by rail to Petersburg where we remain an hour for breakfast, then to Weldon

11.30. It is safe to get some luncheon here, as the probabilities are that you get no more refreshment till you arrive at Wilmington 10 or 11 P.M. When I got to Wilmington, where I intended staying the night, I found that if I continued travelling all night, I should be in Charleston by 8 or 9 o'clock on the following morning. The chances of rest seemed but remote at Wilmington, as the cars left very early in the morning for the day train. So I got some refreshment and kept on my journey, and a tedious one it was. I don't much remember the distance from Richmond to Petersburg, but from there to Charleston (434 miles) it is one interminable forest of pines, only here and there relieved by some few patches being got into cultivation. The stations, excepting two or three towns we pass, are often places merely to take on water and fuel with but two or three log huts, which is a natural consequence, as these through-lines of railway have been cut straight through the forest, irrespective of local circumstances.

This part of North Carolina is called the rosin and turpentine country. The pines are barked for a considerable height for the purpose of abstracting the rosin, which gives them a very bleached appearance. They are sometimes set on fire, when they look like a forest of masts, as they don't burn down to the ground, but have a charred naked look. It is a grand sight to see one of these forests on fire, we passed near one in the night.

After leaving Wilmington (where we cross the water and change cars) we pass through some of the *desolate* swamps. The railways are very unsafe here, being constructed on what they call trestlework, that is piles rudely constructed. Such places in England would be raised with solid earth with culverts for the water courses, but it is not so here. Still, if we consider, it is a grand undertaking to form a line of railway (although only a single track) through forest and swamp such as this, for a distance of 434 miles, almost inaccessible but for that.

The line has been cheaply constructed as the country is flat and timber on the spot in great abundance, land at a low price and no fencing required. When daylight appeared again, we were either crossing a swamp or cutting through the forest. It has a most singular appearance to look back at one of these forests through which we are passing, as the line has, as it were, merely cut its way through, with stately pines on each side, which in the distance almost seem to close in again. We have a different character often on the edge of these swamps. We have left the pines. Here we first see the Southern Moss, which is a very peculiar feature growing from the trees, three to four feet long, and hanging in festoons from tree to tree. It gives the forest a very mournful, sombre look, at the same time very beautiful. You would suppose that it was hanging dead from the trees, but on examination you find that it grows like the trees. The trees are remarkably tall, and on the edges of these swamps have honeysuckle and wild jessamine running up them. The dog tree looks very pretty with its white flowers.

On approaching Charleston we only leave the forest two or three miles before we are in sight of the city. The change seems like magic from such a wilderness, for the last two days' travelling to open out on fertile gardens, abounding in almost tropical vegetation of every description and the greatest luxuriance. It is quite late for peas here now (9th April). Those we had at table today were quite old. Strawberries in abundance. They grow their own figs, oranges and grapes in the open air.

The weather here is very hot, thermometre 86 in the shade. As a long journey generally has an end, so had mine, but I began to be dreadfully tired, having had twenty-eight hours in the cars. Arrived at Charleston at 8 A.M., and proceeded at once to the Mills House, which I found very comfortable. I consider it the best house I have met with in the States. After having had a bath, which is decidedly the best thing after a fatiguing journey, it is no use going to bed if you get in in the morning; I set out to present my letters of introduction to Messrs. Mitchell and Calder, from whom I received the greatest possible kindness and attention during my stay in Charleston. Mr. C took me to his club and entered my name as his friend, which gave me access whenever I was at a loss for amusement and wished to see the newspapers, etc.

In the afternoon I called upon Mr. G. A. Trenholm to whom I also had a letter from Mr. Souter, Bank of the Republic, N. York. He was out of town on his rice plantation twenty miles up the river. Saw his brother, who wished to see me again on Monday, when he could probably make some arrangement for my going up to see his plantation. Piccolomini sings here this evening, too tired to accompany Mr. Calder.

April 10th: Sunday. Attended service with Mr. Calder at the Episcopal Church (St. Michaels) in the morning. Mr. Mitchell in the afternoon was going to attend the opening of a newly erected Presbyterian Church, built especially for the negroes, and capable of holding 2,500 persons. He very kindly asked me to accompany him. It was well filled on the occasion and the services were very interesting, particularly to me, as I had never seen so many black people together. Much struck with the preponderance of blacks present (near 2,000) also the manifest interest they took in the service, and the very orderly manner in which they conducted themselves. They commence singing before the service commences, and when the Minister comes in they sing some of their favourite hymns. After that the service was the same as the Presbyterian Churches in Scotland. Heard a very superior preacher, Mr. Girardeau, was that day specially ordained to preach at that negro church. I afterwards ascertained that he had a much larger stipend offered by the Savannah people to preach there, which he declined, considering himself more in the way of his duty to preach to these poor negroes than to the wealthy planters in Savannah. I was very much pleased with him. In the evening we went to the Wesleyan Methodist Church and afterwards to the Baptist. In all churches in this city, excepting the Episcopalian, there is a certain part set aside for the exclusive use of the negroes, which seats are generally well filled. My object today in visiting so many places of worship was that I probably should not spend another Sunday where I could see so many slaves together (I believe out of a population of 60,000 in Charleston 30,000 are slaves). I was anxious to see how they spent the Sunday, and what religious privileges they enjoyed, and was certainly very favourably impressed with the widest interest they take in the services of the various churches to which they belong. A striking contrast to the free blacks and general white population of the Northern Cities.

Among those 2,000 blacks in Mr. Girardeau's church I noticed many of them take out their Bibles and follow the Minister, and when the service was over (without knowing what was collected) I would rather take the sum than what an average white population in the old country would subscribe. I wish some of our English people, who are very loud in their condemnation of slavery, could see how these *poor blacks* spend their Sunday. They would shame the population of many an English village on a Sunday morning.

April 11th: Called again upon Mr. Trenholm. As his brother was on his rice plantation, twenty miles upriver, and very difficult of access, he thought I should do better by seeing other rice plantations nearer the city, than by spending the time necessary to go up there. Took his advice and Mr. Mitchell very kindly introduced me to his friend

Mr. — at the Bank, who offered if we would wait till Wednesday to take us up to Pimlico to see Col. Gadsden's rice plantation on the Astley river, thirty miles from Charleston, where there are between 200 and 300 negroes. Seeing a slave sale advertised for the following day, I was anxious to witness it, so made our arrangements accordingly.

The wharfs here abound in cotton. The bales are piled up a considerable height and quite exposed to the atmosphere, never under shelter. After the bales come from the planters to a seaport like Charleston, they are compressed by steam power, or they would take up too much space on shipboard. It is a simple process: the covering of the bale, which having been pressed by the machinery on the plantations where it is picked, does not meet by twelve or eighteen inches; after steam pressure this covering considerably overhangs, as you see when the bales arrive in Europe. The Sea Island Cotton (which is a longer fibre) will not bear the process.

The weather now is intensely hot to me; the people living here don't feel it, so the summer heat of this place must be fearful. It is a well-built place, laid out rather more on the English plan than American. Meeting Street is the principal one. There is a famous market for fruits and vegetables.

In the evening I accompanied Mr. Mitchell to a large party (from thirty to forty) at Mr. Porter's and spent a very agreeable evening. I was rather amused by the opinions the Americans, who have not been to Europe, entertain of Eng-

lish people and their country, our Queen, etc. Being introduced by my friend as Mr. Vessey from London, I had
many questions to answer about the old country, got back
to the hotel about 1 o'clock. The evenings here are delight-
fully cool and pleasant after the intense heat of the day.
The Battery is a very pleasant promenade when the sun is
down, with the sea dashing up to the walls, for you are out
on the Atlantic at once. It is a beautiful bay formed by the
junction of the Cooper and Astley rivers, and the Atlantic
is quite within sight.

The country is flat and where it is not under rice culture
is forest. On the opposite side of the bay are the Islands,
which are chiefly used in cultivating the Sea Island Cotton,
equally unhealthy to the White Man as are the Rice
swamps. They are not considered safe, in fact it is said to
be certain death to a White Man to sleep upon a rice plantation after the first of May. The roads are chiefly sand, the
natural soil being light. One half of the road is usually
laid out with planks across, which serve as the best road in
the extreme wet or dry weather, but being heavier draught,
I observe are not preferred if the natural road is at all
passable.

In Bay St. there is a palmetto tree growing; it is looked
upon as a sort of guardian angel of the place. Cotton is the
great article of export from Charleston. All the wharfs are
filled with it, and I suppose that this is not the most busy
season of the year. I don't know the number of bales annually shipped from the port of Charleston, but since my

return to England, I found the following statement in *The Times,* Sept. 14th, 1859:

> *Total receipts for cotton for the year ending Sept. 1st.* Memphis, Tenn., 325,000 bales against 243,000 last year. New Orleans, 1,672,814, increase over last year 100,405. Mobile, 704,000, increase over last year 181,155. Savannah, 676,780, increase over last year 170,000.

Tuesday, April 12th: The Yankees are so used to advertising everything that even when a man dies they give notice through the newspaper to his friends and relatives that they are expected to attend the funeral.

> DIED, on the 11th inst., GEORGE EDWARDS, in the 83rd year of his age. The relatives and friends of the deceased, and those of his son, Dr. George B. Edwards, and of his son-in-law, Ogden Hammond, are requested to attend the funeral services *this afternoon,* at Four o'clock, at Mr. Hammond's residence, Smith Street, second house southwest of Beaufain Street.   April 12

> The Friends and Acquaintances of Mr. and Mrs. John H. Bullwinkle and family are respectfully invited to attend the funeral of their son D. W. BULLWINKLE, from their residence, corner of Mazyck and Magazine Street at Three o'clock this afternoon without further invitation.   April 12

April 12th: Tuesday. Seeing an advertisement in the Charleston Mercury, I attended at Chalmers Street (the slave market) to witness one of these sales.

The yard in which they are exposed for sale is just out

of the public street, at the end of which is a large house, where the slaves are lodged and taken care of. A sort of depot for slaves where there are always some on sale, and where you can purchase one at any time, or at the auctions that take place weekly.

The auctioneer offers them like selling any other goods with the usual conditions, *warranted slaves,* naming their defects if they are unsound. I believe that there is a heavy penalty for any dealer to sell a man who is not a slave. They are all neatly dressed and look well in health.

The first one I saw offered was not bid for (I think a runaway by the look of him) nor the next.

After that a woman and two children, aged respectively two and four years, they made 440 dollars each (1420 dol.)

The next Charles, eighteen years of age; a sharp intelligent boy, he showed no grief about it and made 1,100 dollars.

1 woman, 940 dol.

1 boy, fourteen years of age (Billy), with restrictions that he was not to be sold out of the city of Charleston, made 970 dol. This boy would probably have made 1,200 dol. if he could have been taken to plantation life. I merely mention this to show that humanity sometimes stands before dollars and cents, even among slave holders.

Next a woman and child three years old made 550 dol. each. This woman showed the most grief when she knew that she was bought to go West. Two cutthroat blackguard-looking fellows bought her.

Woman sempstress, lame, 850 dol., observations on this lot by two fellows (nasal twang) "Take that gal to the springs for two months and get her sound, I guess she would fetch 1,200 dollars."

Many other families were offered, some were sold, others withdrawn, the price not being considered sufficient.

I think they look with suspicion upon strangers going into these slave marts. Although no observation was made to me, it was very evident they saw I was not a dealer.

The heat today was very intense and I bought some clothes suitable for such a climate. I also changed some money at the Bank of Charleston 72 dol. 85 cents for £15 English. There is a very good market for vegetables and fruits. Meat is not so good, but that observation applies to all hot countries.

In the afternoon drove to the Magnolia Cemetery, a distance of two or three miles from the city. The natural situation is peculiarly suitable for such a place. The tall trees with the beautiful moss growing from them give it a very funereal appearance. It is on the edge of one of those vast swamps with which the country abounds, where the tide overflows, filling the creeks twice a day, which run in and around the cemetery. If you happen to see it when the tide is up, it is the most appropriate spot for a burying place I ever saw. I noticed the tombs of many denoted only a short life, the fevers here are so fearful.

After leaving the Magnolia we drove to the western side of the city, where with those fronting the Battery are the best residences in Charleston. They are chiefly built of wood, and all have Piazzas or Verandahs around them, which are much used in the hot weather.

I think that the Mills House is the most comfortable hotel in the U.S.

April 13th: Very hot (86 in the shade), kept indoors in consequence. Bought some tobacco, 45 cents per pound, and cigars, sent them to New York to await my arrival.

Left by 3 P.M. train with Mr. Mitchell, Mr. Scriven, Mr. Roper, Mr. Johnson and party to the Strawberry Hill Station on the Florence Railway, twenty-four miles, where two carriages met us, and after a drive of about five miles through the forest came to Pimlico, Col. Gadsden's rice plantation, where we staid all night. It is a good house, built of wood, as all these planters' residences are, and approached by an avenue of fine oak trees. I must confess that I was somewhat nervous at sleeping here, after all that I had heard about the unhealthiness of these rice swamps to the White Man; but Mr. M and all of them assured me there was no danger till the first of May. Although the planters' houses are always built on the high ground, the miasma arising from the swamps is certain death after the hot season sets in. It is not well to go on the rice ground after the sun is down, but as our time was limited, and as the overseer declared there was no occasion for any alarm, we saw the rice grounds near the house that evening before we came in.

It was in various stages of progress from the recently

sown seed upwards. There are many negroes employed here, I believe Col. Gadsden has 226. Their houses are built of wood and whitewashed, and the negroes appear very comfortable and happy. They have a place of worship in the grounds, and the planter maintains a minister to preach to them, which I afterwards found was usual on the larger plantations. The Wesleyan, Methodist and Baptist are the ministers usually preferred by the negroes, particularly the former. I believe they are the only sect who visit the rice swamps after the hot season has set in, it being a requirement on their entering their missionary labours that they should not shrink from it. But few of them fall a sacrifice, of course they only go in the heat of the day when there is not so much danger. On smaller plantations I find the masters generally give the negroes the privilege of attending any place of religious worship they please on a Sunday. The Presbyterians are also numerous among the blacks.

Of the land cleared, the lowlands, such as can be flooded, are under rice, probably two hundred acres on this plantation. The upper land is chiefly under Indian corn, potatoes and some little sugar cane. All sorts of game and wild fowl abound in the woods and some of our party being fond of shooting soon brought back some wild ducks, partridges, quails, etc., some of which we had for supper.

Spent a very agreeable evening and made ourselves very comfortable, drank some of the best Monaghela whisky of the country which the late Col. Gadsden had had in bond in New Orleans I don't know how many years. Among the many anecdotes and adventures told that evening it was very odd that Mr. Mitchell should relate the following respecting the loss of the *Arctic* in which poor Ralph Maddison was lost.

Mr. Mitchell was one of the seventy-six passengers out of three hundred when the *Arctic* was lost Sept. 27, 1854. Twenty-five were saved in the boat in which he was and another boat of twenty kept with them forty-two hours on the water without food or water before they got sight of land. Compass of no use as their boats were of iron, and had not some of the men in the boat espied some land birds which they followed they would probably have never seen land again. See his letters in *The Times*, Oct. 12th to 15th, 1854.

April 14th: Thursday. Up early, and after breakfast (of wild ducks, partridges, corn cakes, etc., and such as you always meet with in the South) took two carriages for a distance of nine or ten miles to other plantations belonging to the same property, to see the like operations in the cultivation of rice. There are more negroes employed here than we saw yesterday. It is very delightful driving through these forests of magnificent timber and abounding in the most beautiful flowers in the wildest luxuriance. I was sorry I could not obtain any seeds of them, it being the wrong season of the year.

Passed a small village and church. Col. Gadsden's overseer, whom I found a very intelligent man (he was with his master the late Col. Gadsden in the taking of the City of Mexico), has to leave the plantation every night during the summer and go away some distance to sleep; now it has quite a contrary effect upon the blacks. The more mud and heat the fatter they become. The negroes on the rice plantations have not so much to do (when the rice is under flood) as on the cotton plantations, excepting cultivating the Indian corn, enough of which is grown for their own consumption and the mules and dogs, although I believe their work is more laborious at times than on the cotton plantations. The system pursued in the rice culture is as follows. After sowing the rice, flood for five or six days till sprouted according to the weather, dry till the seed is up, flood thirty days, then dry to hoe and cultivate for another thirty days. Then flood till the rice is ripe, run the water off to reap it.

A field hand on such rivers as the Cooper, upon which this plantation is situated, cultivates about ten to twelve acres, over six acres under rice and four acres under corn or potatoes. The rice in its primitive state is called "paddy," sells from 85-95 cents to a dollar per bushel and when cleaned of the husk and ready for use commands $1.50 to $2.50 according to quality.

The rice crop on broad rivers is considered a safe crop and will yield on an average from fifty to fifty-five bushels per acre. To cultivate rice to advantage it must be on a large river influenced by the tide but sufficiently above it not to admit the salt water. Of course lands vary in price according to these causes (their situation and productive-

69

ness) and range in value accordingly from $150 to $200 and even $250 per acre.

Much pleased with what I had seen and drove back in time for dinner at Pimlico to catch the evening train, not forgetting a little incident in crossing the Cooper river in the ferry boat where we had nearly been stranded through the incompetence of the niggers who had charge of the ferry; in fact, had it not been for Col. Gadsden's overseer who had a good knowledge of how to cross a strong current with the wind against us and the tide running strong, we should have floated down the river in spite of all the men could have done. We had all to help or we should have never got across. The old nigger who is the proper ferry-man was sick, as they say when a man is ill, so I went to his house to see how they lived. Excepting being black people you would not have known it from a dirty cottage in England. They are not clean people. After a hasty dinner we had but just time to catch the 4.25 train at the Strawberry Station for Charleston. Enjoyed myself most heartily and very sorry to part with such pleasant company. On these plantations in the South they had a most delightful life, when the weather is not *too* hot, surrounded by every luxury a warm climate can produce. A well-managed plantation ought to produce almost all the food requisite for not only the planters house but his negroes, mules, etc. Indian corn, fruit, vegetables, game in abundance. Wheat they can't grow—the climate is too hot. They have a small patch of sugar canes on this property, a plant of which I brought home with me, also some rice (paddy) grown here.

Arrived in Charleston at half past five and immediately drove to the Mills House to receive my letters which Mr. Calder was good enough to meet me with. Great pleasure on receiving my first letter from home since I left and to find that they were all well.

Mr. Mitchell very kindly offered to send me up to Joshe, the largest rice plantation in that neighbourhood, where more than seven hundred negroes are employed, but as it would only be a similar thing on a larger scale I declined, as it would take me more than a week going up and returning.

Very sorry to part with my kind friends Mr. Mitchell and also Mr. Calder, who contributed so much to make my stay in Charleston agreeable. Mr. M gave me a letter to a friend in Chicago. They (Messrs. M and C) have recently purchased a large tract of country in Wisconsin (thirty thousand acres) on speculation.

Left that evening by steamboat (the *Gordon*) for Savannah where we arrived about 4 A.M. the following morning. I think the journey by land takes a day, so of the two evils I thought seasickness for one night on the Atlantic was preferable to a long day in the cars. There is always a considerable swell on the Atlantic, so after a short illness I got off to bed and knew but little of our journey till I found myself in the morning in the port of Savannah.

The boats are very clean and the berths very comfortable.
April 15: Savannah. There is but little rest after our

arrival although it is so early. Everyone is anxious to get their baggage and leave the boat.

I turned out about 6 and left for the Hotel Pulaski. It was so full that there was no chance of getting a room till the first train left at 9 o'clock. I therefore got some paper and wrote home to Barbara to announce my safe arrival so far. After breakfast I called upon Charles Green, Esq. (firm of Andrew Low & Co.), Cotton Brokers. Of course all the great merchants in these Southern Cities are engaged in cotton. He was unfortunately from home in Florida but one of his clerks took me to Col. Jones, Lafayette Square, to whom I also had a letter of introduction. He was on his rice plantation two or three miles out of the city. These planters are on their estates early in the morning and leave by 12 or 1 o'clock, when the sun becomes very powerful. I immediately engaged a carriage and drove over to see him and was very fortunate in finding him there. I found him a very intelligent man, blunt in his manner but with a good share of common sense. He took a very lively interest in everything pertaining to agriculture and the cultivation of rice in particular, and finding that I was not a stranger to the cultivation of land we soon became acquainted.

His rice lands are laid out on a very superior plan to anything I have seen in this country and being naturally higher than what I saw at Col. Gadsden's are much easier of cultivation in many respects. His rice plantation is in fields of from five to ten acres and sown in drills (all by

72

hand labour and as perfectly straight as though done by machinery). It struck me at the time that his drills by hand labour would do credit to any North Lincolnshire drill-man. I suggested to him the use of drills, horse loco, etc., etc., such as we use in England to economise labour. Promised to send him catalogues of implements from some of our best makers, which he appeared to take great interest in as those they have in use are of a very rude description. The rice is in various stages of its growth, from that just up to some six inches high, and Col. J thought he should still sow some. They are troubled with what they call volunteer rice, i.e. the produce of what shook last harvest. Although they can hoe out what comes up between the drills, that in the drills ripens at a different time to that sown in the spring, consequently spoils the sample. The flooding in the autumn will not cause it all to grow. I suggested the broadshare and then flood.

Much pleased altogether with the management and general cultivation of this plantation, which appears to be carried out on a scientific plan. Cut up a growing cane here, with which these rice lands abound, which I kept as a walkingstick through the States and eventually brought back with me to England.

The high lands, as on other plantations, are under Indian corn, potatoes, etc., for the negroes, mules and dogs. I noticed some land under oats which I took for rice, which Col. Jones explained to me was equally suitable for rice culture as what we had seen, but being so near the City of

Savannah the malaria arising from the frequent flooding was thought to be so injurious to the health of the City that a large sum of money was paid to the proprietor of this and adjoining lands within a certain distance of the City in order that it should not be under rice culture.

RICE CULTIVATION AS ADOPTED ON COL. JONES' ESTATE, SAVANNAH

Sow the seed in March or April, 2½ bushels per acre. Flood the land which he calls "the sprout flow," keep on the water till the seed is sprouted, which of course depends upon the heat of the weather, then let it be dry till about 20 days from the first planting. As soon as you can see the rows well, put on the water again, which is called the "point flow", keep it on 30 days, then dry the ground and hoe the rice till it begins to show a joint. Then put on the water, which is called the "harvest flow", keep that on till the rice is ripe, then run the water off to reap it.

Average yield per acre, 50 bushels.

Col. Jones last year had 70 bushels.

Indian corn is sown like turnips in rows 2½ to 3 feet wide and 2 feet apart in the rows. Col. J last year had 50 bushels per acre but he manures his in the ridges like turnips and farms his estate on a very high principle for this country, collecting manure from Savannah which he has for leading. He could hardly be made believe that bones were a stronger manure than such as he got from the stables of the City. He said if it were so he could have any quantity for collecting. I have no doubt he will prove what I told him about the use of bones, as I have not often met with a man more alive to availing himself of circumstance than Col. Jones. After seeing the plantation we came up to the buildings and nigger quarter, where the slaves live. These houses are of wood and neatly whitewashed, as at Col. Gadsden's. The people were all at work in the fields excepting some old women nurses and the young niggers who are not old enough to go out to field work. The planters provide hospitals for the sick and usually a place of worship on the plantation, for after cooking and singing, going to Church stands next with the nigger.

Dined with Col. Jones at his residence in the city, Lafayette Square, and was much surprised to find him so well informed about our drainage, embankments, warping, inclosure and reclamation of waste lands in Lincolnshire and other parts of England—the more so when I found that he had not been into Europe but had obtained his information from works on the subject.

In addition to his rice plantation here he has also a cotton plantation some seventy miles distant, to which he very kindly invited me if I would spend a week with him and go up there, where he employs a large number of people. I have perhaps not made the remark before but you seldom hear the word *slave* in the South. A planter will talk to you of his people, servants, etc. but never slaves.

A slave sale took place on the racecourse of this city about a month back—the largest sale of negroes that has ever

75

taken place here belonging to one man. Below is the description of the sale as taken from the catalogue. The figures attached to each lot were put down at the sale by a gentleman present on whom I can rely and show the manner in which they were sold in families. The figures attached to each denote the average price of each slave in dollars. The brackets show the lots in which they were sold.

PIERCE BUTLER ESTATE

List of 442 Negroes
To be offered at Public Sale at the Race Course near this City on the 2nd March next and on succeeding days until sold by

J. Bryan, Savannah.

Terms of sale—one third cash, the remainder payable in two equal annual instalments bearing interest from the day of sale to be secured by approved Mortgage and personal security or approved acceptances on Savannah or Charleston I.C. Purchasers to pay for papers.
For further enquiry address

J. Bryan, Broker
Johnson Square, Savannah

It would be too tedious to copy the whole catalogue, but those given below are a sufficient index of the manner in which they are classed and sold, together with the prices each lot realized, as witnessed by the gentleman to whom I have referred, who was present at the sale.

Price each
slave made:

Dollars	Name	Age	Remarks
1210	Hector's Bess	42	Cotton hand
	Ben	21	Cotton prime young man
	Betty	17	
	Phoebe	15	
	Hector	12	Fine boy
300	Worster	45	Rice hand
	Mary	40	Cotton hand
600	Commodore Bob	aged	Rice hand
	Kate	–do–	Cotton
	Linda	19	Cotton prime young woman
	Joe	13	Rice prime boy
1135	Bob	30	Rice hand
	Mary	25	Rice prime woman
250	Anson	49	Rice ruptured one eye
	Violet	55	Rice hand
475	Allen Jeffrey	46	Rice hand and sawer in steam mill
	Sukey	43	Rice hand
	Watty	5	
645	Rina	18	Rice prime young woman
	Samuel	1	

77

Dollars	Name	Age	Remarks
585	Pompey	31	Rice lame in one foot
	Kitty	30	Rice prime woman
	Pompey Junior	10	Prime boy
	John	7	
	Noble	1	Boy
650	Andrew	45	Lame in right hand, cough—Blacksmith
	Hetty	42	Rice hand
	Lena	12	Prime girl
	Covington	10	Prime boy

April 16: Saturday. Here I was obliged to make up my mind about Cuba, whether I should visit Havana or not, but the increased heat as I journeyed South together with the state of my health, which was far from good, caused me reluctantly to give it up, which, I have no doubt, was the most prudent course as it was getting too late for a tropical climate.

Very unwell at Savannah. The heat of yesterday in viewing Col. Jones's rice plantation too much for me. Staid quietly at the hotel. Rainy morning, quite a refreshing sight where everything is like a side oven. It is about the second time I have seen rain since I arrived in the country.

The markets here are most liberally supplied with fruits, vegetables, etc. The City of Savannah is more like a Dutch town with the trees on each side of the street, only that it is built in squares—in many streets there are double rows of trees. It is a fearful place for dust as there is no material on the roads, which are composed of loose sand. Although it stands higher than many American cities, being on a considerable elevation above the river, I should not take it to be a healthy place—in fact, my experience did not lead me to think so as I was never well during my stay.

A stranger (from Europe) can't but be struck with the absence of poverty in these American cities. I could pick up more waste cotton on the wharfs in Charleston or Savannah in two hours than would keep a family in England a week.

April 17: Called upon Mr. Green at his residence, Madison Square. Accompanied him to his Church (Presbyterian). Very good congregation. Met a lady at his house who returns by the *Persia* on 25th May. After church, called again upon Col. Jones to have some further conversation with him about the cultivation of rice. He much wished me to remain tomorrow to see another rice plantation twenty-five miles off, where he promised to take me. Sorry I had to decline as time would not admit, having so much before me to see, and another rice plantation would merely be a repetition of what I had seen at his place and Col. Gadsden's.

They (his family) were very inquisitive whether I was going to write a book about their country as I was so particular about every detail in connection with the rice cultivation. They are very zealous of what foreigners think of them, particularly the English.

In the afternoon found a niggers' church where a black

man preached to a black congregation, which was very large, but that observation applies to all the churches I have attended in the South. Drank tea at Mr. Green's and in the evening accompanied them to their church.

Taken very ill again in the night. Sent a note to Mr. Green who very kindly came down to the Pulaski Hotel to see me. Consulted his physician, Dr. Arnold, who relieved me. He thought the water did not agree with me, which is so often the case with strangers. I would advise anyone unaccustomed to the water of these Southern or Western cities never to drink it pure without either spirits or something to take off that effect.

They have no artesian wells, consequently the water is generally thick. Very glad to have Dr. Arnold's opinion what was the best thing to take and what to avoid, as I had taken a deal of quinine during the time I had been visiting the rice plantations, knowing how unhealthy they are, and was afraid it might have been the commencement of one of the fevers the people of this country are so subject to.

April 18: Dr. Arnold rather recommended me to leave Savannah if I felt well enough to travel, which was far from satisfactory, when a doctor tells you the place does not agree with you.

However, I took his advice and left by the 12.15 train after changing some money at Mr. Green's bank, and arrived at Augusta, Ga., about 5 P.M. Planters House. I enter this merely to show the style of hotels away from the great cities.

April 19: Augusta is a small inland town with one main street through the place, very wide and planted with trees on each side. If the weather be dry it is dirt, if wet, mud, for like most other American towns the streets are what nature made them. Weather intensely hot.

Called upon Messrs. Miller and Manen who (as Mr. M was from home, who has a cotton plantation) introduced me to Mr. McGruder living twenty-five miles off, who has an extensive farm and grows a considerable quantity of corn and cotton and employs many slaves. He was good enough to ask me to see his place, and as he could not see me till the following day he recommended me to take the cars to Berzelea that afternoon, stay at Kirkpatrick's and take a wagon on in the morning to his place about five or six miles distant.

Left Augusta by the 2.30 train for Berzelea station according to his instructions. On alighting from the train I found one solitary house in the forest surrounded by a good garden, but whether it was a private house, an inn or a railway station I was in some doubt, but the train having gone on I went up and explained my object in alighting there.

Two men live here, Messrs. Kirkpatrick and Leitner, intelligent shrewd men, who farm very extensively, keeping seventy-five mules for draught purposes.

In addition to their farming they have a steam sawmill which I have often wondered are not more common here among such magnificent timber, particularly as the railways have opened out a market to these previous inaccessible forests.

Mr. L was very civil to me and showed me over his place. He has laid out grounds with some taste which some day, when the young trees get up, will form a pleasing picture to his residence, having dammed up the stream in the valley below, which will be seen from the house, when he gets the intervening forest cleared. He had seen an eagle hovering about and was going out with his gun and asked me to accompany him. We were not successful, but I was not in condition to walk far in the forest so returned and spent the evening in seeing the slaves plough among the vines and watermelons near the house. Old Kirkpatrick returned from his farm in the evening and was quite sorry that he had not been at home when I arrived, as he would have been glad to have shown me their farm, which I afterwards saw the following day.

They do not grow much cotton although the land is suitable, and the climate particularly so. Corn and wheat are more value to them in their business than inferior cotton which their land, being poor, would only produce. Their wheats are now (April 19) in full ear and flower. Had much conversation with them about agriculture in England which much interested them as their cultivation of corn and cotton interested me. They have a large number of blacks—many of them are employed in their sawing mills and building operations. I noticed some of them at work (carpenters) who seemed as skilled in their trade as any white man in a similar business in England would be. They have usually an acre or two of watermelons on these places. Vines grow in the open; also peaches, apples, plums, etc., etc., are as common as blackberries. They consider one field hand (i.e. nigger) and one mule = to about twenty acres of land under corn or cotton. The corn is planted four feet apart and two feet in the rows. They cultivate by continuous ploughing between the rows, hoeing what the plough does not reach. The wheats are light, I think the land and climate too hot for wheat. I notice the overseer rides on horseback among the people and continues with them all day. The cotton seed is very valuable as a manure—one handful being sufficient to force a stalk of Indian corn. It is a great peculiarity in these forests that when the pine is cut down oaks spring up spontaneously, and vice versa.

The same observation has repeatedly been made to me while passing through them. The people were very kind and we spent a pleasant evening after the labours of the day were over, but of all the wild places under heaven this certainly was the wildest place I ever spent a night in during my travels. Picture to yourself one solitary house in a dense forest of the most magnificent timber you ever saw, near to which is a sort of dependence, as we should call it in Switzerland, but here the lower part was used as sort of store, the upper part as bedrooms, in one of which I was obliged to sleep as the house proper was undergoing repair. In the background of this place were a lot of nigger huts.

83

It certainly appeared to me as the last place in creation but there was no help but to stay the night.

After supper such as the country affords, I turned off to bed but I can't say to much sleep, as I did not much like my quarters, in addition to which the nights are so intolerably hot in these latitudes.

April 20: Not sorry when daylight appeared to get up and breakfast at half past 5 and leave at 6 with a nigger boy and waggon to Mr. Magruder's, a distance of five or six miles. We leave the forest after a mile or two, where we open out on Mr. Kirkpatrick's farm. Their foreman was ready to meet me and show me over the place. He got me some cotton seed which I brought to England. The trees are the largest I ever saw. They generally attach ten mules (and theirs are the best cattle of the kind I ever saw) to one tree to bring it to the sawmill. Met many of their teams on the way which the lad said belonged to his masters. He seemed much attached to them and I must observe in justice to the slave holders generally that it is the feeling I have usually found among the slaves in this class towards their owners.

Passed through many cotton fields on the way to Mr. M's. Arrived at his house about 8. It was the most intensely hot day I ever experienced. At 6 o'clock in the morning when we left Berzelea I felt the benefit of my umbrella, and during the day at Mr. Magruder's the heat was most oppressive (Fahr. 123). I found Mr. M ready on my arrival, for the people are up early here.

After inspecting his premises he showed me the process the cotton undergoes in "ginning," which is a machine like a number of blunt saws which separate the cotton from the seed. It is then packed in bales of 500 lbs. weight each. But all planters do not make their bales the same uniform weight but the larger ones always make 500 lbs. to a bale. It is then pressed with such machinery as they possess on the plantation and sent off to the seaports. Afterwards it undergoes the process of steam pressing as seen in Charleston previous to shipment to Europe.

Mr. M's cotton is not so forward as some we saw on other plantations we visited, some of which was a second leaf. Saw many negroes at work here and at other plantations. The women hoe the cotton chiefly, the men ploughing with a mule and vice versa—a woman appears to me to do about as much work as a man. Although the weather is so hot the negroes seem to delight in it. When they get their dinner they never get into the shade as we should suppose, but delight to bask in the hot sun. You will often see a nigger asleep with the full glare of sun upon him, the temp. ranging from 100 to 120, which would drive any white man mad.

The planters have all about the same quantity of land under cultivation per field hand on such land as this, which is a poor soil—probably eight acres of cotton and twelve acres of corn per field hand and mule. The average yield of this district would perhaps not exceed five bales of cotton per field hand. Middle Georgia, which is a better district, would probably produce eight bales to the field hand, where you might reverse the order of cultivation, i.e. twelve acres of cotton and eight corn. In the spring of the year the cotton planter pitches his crop as he calls it, i.e. considering the condition and number of his mules and slaves, he calculates how much cotton he can grow (which is the valuable crop, as he only grows Indian corn, potatoes, etc., for the use of his establishment and not for sale).

A hundred bushels of corn is the usual allowance per annum for each mule.

Fifteen bushels for each negro, with 150 lbs. bacon (with a small patch of land, which is usually given them on the best plantations, which fills him full of pocket money for missionary enterprize, tobacco, or any other luxury they may feel inclined to indulge in). I say missionary as I have myself witnessed the manner they give at the Churches.

After making these arrangements the planter keeps as much under corn as will feed his hogs and poultry, which are a very important item as the niggers won't eat any other meat but bacon.

PROCESS OF COTTON CULTIVATION

The seed is sown in March or April in rows 4 feet apart and singled out like turnips in the rows. The land between is constantly ploughed. The hoeing and cultivation goes on till July, the latter end of which month it begins to ripen, when they commence gathering the pods which will keep bearing till the frost sets in. Cotton blossoms in June—white flower the first day—and does not open till the sun is up. Red flower the second day and falls off the third. Sea Island Cotton flowers yellow and changes to pink.

The planters' houses are built of wood and painted white. They have a peculiar light, airy look, well adapted for such a hot climate. They have all good orchards attached to their places, which I generally found to be the best fenced place on the premises, and on enquiry ascertained it was for the purpose of turning in the hogs to pick up the fallen fruit. I never saw peaches grow in such abundance before as in Mr. Magruder's orchard. The trees are all standards and the fruit as thick as blackberries. You never see the English gooseberry or currant—I suppose like the white-thorn the soil or climate does not suit them.

Saw many little negroes at Mr M's in the nigger quarter. They seemed very happy and contented. They are always in charge of some old nurse woman who is unfit for field labour.

After spending a most delightful day with Mr. M and obtaining much valuable information about the cultivation of cotton I was sorry to part with my friend and his family, from whom I had received so much kindness.

Since writing the above on the spot I met with the accompanying paragraph in a Charleston paper which in so many respects confirms what I have said about plantation life. I thought it not out of place to enter it:

As cotton is the principal staple of production, as well as of conversation, a little statistical information concerning it may prove interesting to your readers. The month of April is the season for planting. The gathering commences the latter part of August, and is continued through the fall months. After the cotton is gathered it is passed through a gin mill to free it from all impurities, and then packed in bales of 400 pounds each. Twelve hundred pounds of cotton to the acre, or five bales to the field hand, is considered an acreage yield in this State. The cost of supporting a slave on these plantations is almost nominal. He will grow fat, and bless you every day, on thirteen bushels of corn and 150 pounds of bacon per year, and five dollars, judiciously expended, will supply him for the same length of time with all the clothing he requires. As the average price of cotton is ten cents per pound, or forty dollars per bale, the profitableness of slave labor can be seen at a glance.

My impressions as to the unfortunate condition and cruel treatment of the slaves have been wholly dissipated by what I have seen during my visit here. My opportunities for visiting the rice plantations in the lower, and the cotton fields in the upper part of the State, have been ample and satisfactory. After giving the subject personal attention, although you may have all the proclivities and bitter prejudices of the North, you will probably arrive at the same conclusion that I did—namely, that the less you put on the back of a slave, the more pork you put in his stomach, and the deeper you can get his feet into the mud, the healthier, fatter, and happier he will be. The rice plantations are usually located in the low lands, or on the banks of the creeks and rivers, in order to secure the advantages of frequent irrigation at stated intervals—something the nature of the plant seems to require. In these localities the miasmatic atmosphere is almost certain death to the white man, while the negro is as certain to thrive in it. Mud and malaria are no objectionable features to him.

Give him his customary rations of bacon and corn meal —beef and mutton he will reject—and he will perform his day's labor cheerfully; and when night comes you will find him in his cabin, playing on the violin or banjo, with Dinah and numberless little picaninnies dancing around him.

Slavery in this State, at least, is of the patriarchal form, and by this expression I do not wish to be understood as insinuating that the head of a family is connected by paternal ties to his slaves, but that he has a fatherly care over them, and otherwise kindly treating them, and finally, when he dies, transmitting them to his children.

Everywhere I have been I have seen the most marked affection displayed on the part of the slave toward his master. A gentleman whose cotton plantation I visited in the upper part of the State told me, as showing the confidence he reposed in his slaves, and their affection for and fidelity to him, that last year they gathered, cleaned, and packed all his cotton without his being obliged to visit his plantation during the season, and not a pound of cotton was wasted, nor a kernel of corn stolen. At the North such implicit confidence as he displayed would be considered, in the language of Uncle Tom's Cabin, "so shiftless!" Calling to one of his field hands, I inquired if he would not like to go to New York with me, and see something of a different life from that he was leading. "No sah," he replied, "dis child ain't g'wine to leave

Massa; 'sides habent got de time—mus make a big crop of cotton for him dis year, sure."

Nor are the spiritual wants of the negroes unsupplied. In Charleston, Mr. Girardeau, a man of fine talent, has a congregation composed almost exclusively of negroes under his charge and in other cities, and, indeed, throughout the whole State, the slaves on Sunday have the same privileges which their masters enjoy.

I mention these *facts*—for *facts* they are—not as an apology for slavery, but for the purpose of correcting some of the many mistaken impressions that prevail among us in regard to it.

The political papers of the day are much to blame for keeping up such a bitter agitation on the subject; for distorting and misrepresenting the facts in the case, and for strengthening those deep-rooted prejudices which so unhappily exist between the people of the North and South. A long and glowing article from *Doesticks*, published in the *New York Tribune* a few weeks since, in regard to the great slave sale at Savannah, was much more calculated to do harm than good, because it was a one-sided statement. As I was present at the sale in question, I may be permitted to state that *Doesticks*, as usual drew largely upon his imagination, and that his report was, in many particulars, not only highly colored but grossly exaggerated. The fact is, he was required to get up a sensation article for an abolition journal, and, like a faithful *slave*, he performed his duty to the best of his ability.

It is but just that I should say that the Southern people have some unfounded prejudices against us, which they will in time, no doubt, overcome. They are especially severe upon the good people of Massachusetts. Gently insinuate, in the mildest manner, that all the natives of that State are not ranting, roaring, hot-headed abolitionists, that there may be a few people there who care less for cotton than they do for codfish, more for ninepence than for a South Carolina negro, and you might sooner expect to find a pair of elephants inspired by the musical notes of a thousand bullfrogs, dancing a friendly *polka-redowa* on the highest peak of the Alleghany Mountains, than to meet with a man here who would be willing to acknowledge the truth of your proposition.

An exchange of visits between the people of the North and South would entirely do away with their illiberal opinions of each other, and soften that spirit of bigotry and intolerance which threaten the peace and prosperity of the Union.

Let me bear testimony that the planters of South Carolina, as a class, at least, are very different men from what they are supposed to be by many people even in our own enlightened State. Instead of being coarse, selfish, cruel, tyrannical, and uncultivated in heart and intellect, they are uniformly intelligent, warm-hearted, indulgent to their slaves, courteous both at home and in their business transactions, and what is a noticeable feature, destitute of that grasping, avaricious spirit which is so often seen among the commercial men of the North. As for their wives and daughters—God bless them—they are not wanting in that winning hospitality, that beauty, grace, and refinement for which the home circles of the sunny South are so eminently distinguished.

The slaves on these plantations were much harder worked than others I had seen. I was glad to have this opportunity of meeting them, as I might have formed a wrong impression of slave life by merely visiting the wealthy class of planters only.

Arrived at Berzelea in time for the evening train for Atlanta, which we reach about 12 P.M. Very hot in the cars. Met with a very intelligent man living in Texas. He described that country as very suitable for the production of long-wool sheep, which I have heard before. I should have thought the climate too hot, but he persisted in it in spite of my arguments against it and he knew what he was talking about. Having the opportunity of staying the night at Atlanta and leaving by the 10 A.M. train, I did so as it was then a thirty hours' uninterrupted run to Memphis. The distances here are so great that I never lost an opportunity of staying the night, when I could do so.

Atlanta Planters House was a small inland town growing fast like most places in this country. The railway runs through the principal street, which is nothing uncommon to me now. The stores recently erected are substantial and well built, but that observation applies to most of these new towns in America. Wherever the original wooden house has to make way for a new store or house, it is built on a very superior scale to what you see in the old country.

Determined here not to go further South as the weather was getting very hot and I was far from well, although I had many valuable letters of introduction through Georgia, Alabama, etc., to planters there, but on consideration I came to the conclusion that I should only see cotton in a rather more forward stage of its growth, the system of cultivation being the same throughout, and under any case I could only see it in its early stages of growth at this season of the year.

Left Atlanta at 10 A.M. for Memphis (fare $16.50). The country for the first twenty or thirty miles is more undulating, better farmed and better land than anything I have seen since I arrived in this country—has more the appearance of land in England if you could substitute whitehorn hedges for the monotonous snake fence so common here. The line is on viaducts in many places which appear to be but slenderly built of timber. They go very slowly over them, which is highly necessary. Many such valleys in England would be filled with earthwork on our railways. They don't check baggage beyond Chattanooga, where we change cars and get our supper. There is great trouble and delay here about the baggage.

We are now leaving the forward vegetation of the South —foliage backward, trees hardly in full leaf. The cars are terribly full and unpleasant for although smoking is not allowed chewing is, which is infinitely more disgusting. Very wet night, altogether the most uncomfortable travelling I have experienced. There are no sleeping cars on this line, in the absence of which they ought to offer greater accommodation to through passengers on a journey of upwards of eight hundred miles, which I believe it is from Savannah to Memphis. At daybreak (April 22) we were passing through large cotton fields in Alabama between

93

Huntersville and Tuscumbia. People just turning out to work. It appears to be good land and well cultivated. The cotton is very good to see in the rows like turnips. After leaving this, which continues for many miles, we pass through a small portion of the state of Mississippi which appears to be poor land, chiefly forest. The line of railway appears to have been but recently formed as the stations are often placed where there is but little population, and the houses and stores look new. It is but a thinly peopled country for many miles. We stay to breakfast at Tuscumbia at 9 A.M. which we began to think long of not having halted for refreshments since 7 o'clock last night at Chattanooga.

Many of our passengers were planters having slaves with them but they were in another car—that is the only distinction in this free and enlightened country. The nigger is not allowed to ride with his master. The blacks ride by themselves—there is but one class for everyone else.

Met with some very intelligent planters who, when they found I was not a novice about the growth of cotton, gave me much information about it and also the value of land in their various localities, as cotton is the only topic of conversation in these parts.

Texas—Fourteen acres under cotton to the field hand and mule and six acres under corn, producing eight bales of cotton to the field hand. Value of such land from $10 to $40 per acre. One hand will pick from 250 to 350 lbs. cotton per day. One mule is worth $150.

Col. Smith, a large planter in Texas, told me in New

York the other day that he will this year grow eleven bales of cotton to the field hand, but this is an exceptional crop.

Take a bale of cotton weighing 500 lbs. at from 10 to 12 cents per lb., 35 bushels of seed, 24 lbs. per bushel. Valuable as a manure, 15 to 20 cents per bushel. Indian corn from 75 cents to $1 per bushel. It requires but little calculation from the above statement to ascertain the value of a field hand with land at a nominal price. Therefore it must be clear to the meanest capacity to see that so long as cotton maintains its present value and labour so high, it is monstrous to talk of the abolition of slavery in the Southern States of America. It is all very well for Exeter Hall people to rave about but I have seldom met with those who have gone down South and seen slavery as it is but have come back with very different views on the subject. For my own part I confess I was under the impression before seeing it that slavery would some day be abolished but after what I have seen I have arrived at a very different conclusion.

Cane-brake land in Alabama

Probable capital required on a cotton plantation employing 50 field hands:—

100 hands—50 field hands at an average of $600 each	$60,000
2,500 acres land at $15 per acre	30,750
25 mules at $175 each	4,375
Wagons, carts, ploughs, etc.	500
	$95,625

besides fodder for the mules first year—30,000 lbs. at 60 cents per cwt. 6,000 bushels corn 75 cents per bushel, food for slaves, mules, etc.

Probable yield of such land 10 bales to the hand—£6,250 a year on a capital of £19,125.

Arrived at Memphis April 22nd 4 P.M. after a thirty hours uninterrupted run. Very tired. Staid at the Gagoso House. Very good hotel facing the great Mississippi, and my room had a most charming view of it with its constant succession of steamboats passing up and down.

My first impression of the great "Father of Waters" was somewhat disappointing. There is nothing grand in the scenery, the banks being flat and, as those accustomed to seeing large rivers well know, they never appear so wide as they are. There is only the satisfaction of knowing that you have before you the largest river and the longest inland water communication in the world. I think the river here is upwards of one and a half miles wide. It is much wider higher up at the junction of the Ohio at Cairo.

April 23: Memphis. How these people have mixed up the ancient with modern names! Perhaps you pass Jackson Villa, Huntersville, then find Rome, Athens, Moscow, Florence, etc., as names of stations. Those who changed those fine old Indian names for those I have just given must have been sad barbarians, as some of the Indian names of the Southern rivers will show:

Tallahasee	Oostanoula	Coosawattee	Etowah
Tallapoosa	Chattahoochee	Chattanooga, etc.	

Presented a letter to Messrs. Candu Mix & Co. who introduced me to many planters in Arkansas (the other side of the river), also to Mr. Orgill, an Englishman residing here (firm of Lownes, Orgill & Co.) who came from Staffordshire. Went to see some slave repositories where slaves are always on sale. The notices below are such as you commonly see in the papers here although they may seem strange to English eyes:

MEMPHIS:
Monday Morning, April 18, 1859—

Negroes for Sale

Just received, seventy-five Virginia and South Carolina *Negroes*, House Servants and Field Hands

DELAP & CO.
Adams-st., between Main and Second.

FIFTY CAROLINA AND GEORGIA NEGROES

Just arrived, for sale in block, for cash or good city acceptances. Call at No. 195 Gravier street.

C. F. HATCHER'S

$100 REWARD

Will be paid for the apprehension of LONDON, with proof to convict any person of harboring him; or I will give $50, if delivered at my office. London ran off about the 24th December last; and formerly belonged to Mr. W. E. Screven, of this city—has a wife at the plantation of Maj. A. Porter, Liberty county, is about 40 or 45 years of age, black, about 5 feet 7 or 8 inches high, and weighs about 140 lbs.

J. BRYAN, Johnson's square.

Mr. M. took me to Forest's depot.

A. & T. FOREST, SLAVE DEALERS (sign over the door).

Found many planters there although it was not a public auction day. On our entering they ring a bell to call the Negroes up out of a yard where they spend their time. If you wish to purchase one or more the planter calls them out of the row and the questions generally put to them are the following: What is their age. What they weigh. Where they have been raised. How much cotton they can pick in a day. Whether they have ever run away. Etc., etc.

When a bargain is struck the dealer draws out a warranty just like selling a house, that *Moses Ephraim Jacob* as the case may be (they are great people for Scripture names) *is a slave* and answers the description given which is the purchaser's title to his bargain.

It is a most revolting sight to witness a slave market in this Western country, far worse than in the South. The people here speak of niggers and I have no doubt treat them in the most unfeeling, ruffianly manner.

A planter came in when I was at either Forest's or De-lap's—I forget which—and asked price of a boy about 14. $1000. "Ah, that is too much. Get another to match him at $800 apiece. I'll call again on Monday." (Just all this in their nasal twang.) He then walks up to Mr. Mereweather with whom I was (another planter) and says, "He would make a good Mississippi bottom boy." Of course we nodded assent, but what a Mississippi bottom boy was I had not the remotest idea. It does not do to say one word about slavery in these parts where bowie knives and revolvers settle all disputes. They don't even entertain the idea that slavery is wrong. They would go great lengths here to maintain it. They are a very different class of people to those I met as planters in South Carolina and Georgia.

In passing through the slave markets I was asked by many slaves to buy them, poor things. I did pity them to be under such wretches in the shape of humanity as some I saw.

On the Lower Mississippi the sugar plantations are usually sold together with the slaves, mules and general stock in one lot as shown below:

VALUABLE PLANTATION AND SLAVES AT AUCTION

By Palfrey & Co.—C. L. C. Dupuy, Auctioneer—Office: 27 Camp Street. Will be sold at auction on *Friday*, April 1, 1859, at 12 o'clock, M., at Banks's Arcade, New Orleans.

The Oakland Plantation, situated in the Parish of Plaquemines, on the right bank of the Mississippi river, 35 miles below the city of New Orleans, with Slaves and Stock, to the highest bidder. The property measures 52 arpents front on the Mississippi river, by a depth between parallel lines of 40 arpents. The improvements comprise a good sugarhouse, cane sheds, two sets of kettles, West Point engine, draining machine, negro cabins, stables, dwellinghouse, etc. etc. There are 650 arpents in cultivation, of which 240 are in plant cane and 200 in rattoons. There are on the estate 53 Kentucky mules, 25 work oxen, 23 cows, 2 bulls, 9 head young stock and 44 head sheep, and the following described slaves:

1. Charlotte, aged 23 years, field hand.
2. Liddy, aged 18 years, field hand, diseased.
3. Sarah, aged 14 years, field hand.
4. Little Jim, aged 9 years, sickly.
5. Herry, aged 27 years, ruptured.
6. Roy, aged 28 years, ruptured.
7. Robert Moore, aged 40 years, gardener.
8. Little Mary, aged 38 years, field hand.
9. Randall, aged 21 years, plowman.
10. Fanny, aged 46 years, field hand.

and so on up to 132.

The whole will be sold in block, exclusive of 600 cords of ash wood and the provisions which may be on the place at the time of sale. These last will be sold separately.

The terms of sale are one fourth cash, and the balance on a credit of one, two, three, four and five years from the date of sale, by notes bearing 6 per cent interest per annum, and 8 per cent eventual interest secured by special mortgage on the property sold and subject to the approval of the vendors.

For further particulars, apply to the Auctioneers, or to
W. & J. MONTGOMERY
149 Common street.

There was so much land flooded on the opposite side of the river in Arkansas that I did not cross in consequence, although I had many invitations to the cotton plantations there. If the flood continues much longer there will be great damage done by not getting the cotton seed sown in proper time. The accounts from the lower Mississippi are very bad and there is great apprehension of the river breaking in many places, as it continues to rise daily.

Memphis is an improving place and well built on a bluff (i.e. high rising ground) facing the river. Everything new is built on a superior scale equal to anything of the kind in one large town in England. The time will come when it will be a very large place, when the railways are more fully developed, as it is surrounded by a fertile cotton country on each side of the river, which is *the* great communication to New Orleans. Even now as at Atlanta you see a magnificent store rising by the side of a wooden shanty which probably ten or fifteen years ago was not considered a bad sort of house when the Red Indians were more common than they are now in these parts. I was so sorry to find that a tribe of Red Indians had been in Memphis only the day before I arrived vending their buffalo skins, etc., as in these remote districts you see them more in their original character than further eastward.

The levee (what would be called a wharf in England) on the river is covered with bales of cotton, all exposed. A stranger would either think it never rained or that cotton was not of much value. The increased annual export of cot-

ton from this place is very great. I have no doubt of its
some day being a large city. There is a great trade on the
river. Steamers constantly up and down. Cotton seems to be
their principal freight—passengers they only take as a side
line—in fact they, before the railways, had the monopoly,
and those going down to New Orleans or up to St. Louis
had no alternative but the river. I saw two steamers leave
for Vicksburg, one waiting for the other to start fair and
have a race. They are such a rascally set for so long as they
have insured the boat they care precious little for their own
lives or those of their passengers, only that they can get to
New Orleans at such a time, for if coals won't do they think
nothing of piling on tar bands and placing a nigger on the
safety valve. In England we should hang such devils, until
we got some honest men to drive the boats. It takes about
four days down the river to New Orleans from here and
five up. There is not so much difference between the up or
down journey although the current is very strong, as going
down they stop to take in fuel by the way, but in going up
the stream they attach the boats having the fuel to the great
steamer which, when they have filled, they let go while
the current quickly takes her back to her moorings ready
for the next steamer.

I consider Memphis to be particularly well laid out in a
sanitary point of view. The main streets are crossed at right
angles, cutting it into blocks, through the centre of which is
a narrow passage sufficient to clear away the refuse from
every house without coming into the main street. I don't

mean to say that this plan obviates dirt in the main streets in Memphis—for what American town is clean?—but in any new town in England it would be a very first-rate plan of building houses.

The great peculiarity in these mushroom cities is that notwithstanding these good houses and stores, if they have made a foot pavement at all it is of wood. The main street is as nature left it, mud axletree deep if the weather be wet, or sand, as the case may be. It is very characteristic of the people—the Americans get a city built leaving the roads and such minor details to another generation.

Much surprised to find that Mr. M (Candu, Mix & Co., a firm carrying the chief business here) had never seen a Bank of England note. I showed him one, which I could see he looked upon as quite a curiosity. Very glad that I had not occasion to change one in these Western parts as I have no doubt it would have been looked upon with great suspicion. He showed me in return what I had often heard of but did not think they were so much in use, viz. a bowie knife and revolver. Laws they have, but these are the policemen who carry them out. I take it these articles carry with them greater weight in these Western Wilds than any decrees from Washington. I don't like the people here at all. The farther you get West, every man for himself and the devil take the last seems to be their motto.

Received letters from home this afternoon (forwarded from Charleston) which gave me very great pleasure, as I suppose I am now the furthest point from England that I shall be.

April 24: Sunday. Called upon Mr. Orgill and accompanied him to the Episcopal Church. In the afternoon Mr. Nevins called upon me at the Gagoso and we went to see the St. Nicholas steamboat preparing to leave for New Orleans. Inspected the saloon and berths—very clean and comfortable. Many beasts on board for New Orleans and general cargo. Saw her leave at 4 o'clock. Wrote to Mr. Mitchell to fix our meeting at New York 25th May.

April 25: As so many plantations were flooded in Arkansas and lower Mississippi by the sudden rising of the river, I determined not to go there as the cotton planting must be in a very backward state, but visit Mr. Mereweather to whom I had a letter from Mr. Brown. Took the early train on the Ohio and Mississippi railroad to the Union Station about twenty miles. On my arrival at the station I enquired if there was any horse or conveyance to take me on. You might as well ask for a camel whilst they are getting in their cotton, and as to post horses the country does not impress a stranger that a great business is carried on in that line. As nothing was to be got of any kind, I had to set out on foot through the forest after making the most minute enquiries as to where Mr. M resided—three miles distant. The stationmaster declared that I could not get wrong as I should not see another house on the way till I got to Mr. M's. This is certainly among the Wilds of the West. There is a degree of grandeur and solemnity in traversing these forests, which have stood since time began. The timber is such as I never saw the like of. There is nothing to break the monotony. The birds, although beautiful in plumage, do not sing. You now and then hear a screeching jay which will make you start. I had not got far before I found the dead body of a hog across the rails. No doubt killed by the train. After walking for near an hour I began to look out for a likely place where a planter might reside. I at last turned off the line through some more open woodland and was fortunate to find it the way up to Mr. Mereweather's place, who I found at home. "Jessamine" is the name of the place. He has about 1200 acres of land—800 cleared and under cotton and corn. He has lately purchased it and removed from Texas, where he has more than 22,000 acres of land for sale and the bulk of his slaves.

The cotton culture here and on other plantations in the neighbourhood he took me to is very similar to what I had seen elsewhere and have before described, only more backward as the climate is colder; I should think on that account not so productive. He gave $16,000 for this estate.

After a very pleasant morning ride on a Texian saddle and horse—a kind of Spanish saddle high on the pummel with a hook in the front—and dining with him, we rode through another part of his property back to the station. We passed through the finest forest of timber I ever saw in my life. Plucked some cotton pods, the remnant of last year's growth which had remained on the bushes.

Very much shocked to find on my arrival at Memphis in

the evening that the St. Nicholas steamboat which we yesterday saw leave for New Orleans had blown up on the river last night and killed 60 people, besides scalding many others who would probably not survive—the more so as she was recommended to me as a safe boat and Mr. Orgill had so strongly urged me not to leave this part of the country without going down to New Orleans, which I found would take four days down, five or six days up with a reasonable time—these would occupy a fortnight. I thought I could spend the time with greater advantage and pleasure in the North so declined with some reluctance, but what a providence there is in these things. Had I done so, I should probably never have been here to tell the tale.

It created quite a gloom through the place when the next upward steamer brought in all the dead bodies picked up with many survivors. I suppose if they even inhale the steam in these cases they never survive for long. The moment a boat blows up they are on fire at once.

April 26: Left Memphis by 7 A.M. train for St. Louis. It is the same line I was on yesterday to Mr. Mereweather's. Passed his place and threw out of the window first published account of the disaster on the river. Wonder whether he ever picked it up. It is almost an uninterrupted forest of magnificent timber to Humbolt, where we change cars at the junction taking us on another line to Columbus, where we take the steamboat up the river to Cairo.

Humbolt Junction. To an English traveller accustomed to an important junction on an English line having refreshment and waiting rooms and everything to make travelling agreeable, what a contrast do these junctions on a newly made line in the forest present! Here in a dense forest with no more timber cleared than is necessary for the line with two sidings at the station to allow trains to pass, with a small log hut or shanty for the man who has charge of the place, passengers alight and await the arrival of the next train exposed to the weather, let it be what it may—fine weather, rain or snow. It is very amusing to watch character on such occasions. Some take it quietly and sit on the stumps and smoke a pipe, others abusing the line and everything in connection with it (but not if he finds you to be an Englishman or foreigner. You never find a Yankee pulling his own country to pieces before a foreigner. On the other hand he declares it is the finest country under heaven with the fastest steamboats, longest railroads, highest mountains and biggest rivers); others amuse themselves in various ways till the train comes up, which is not always very punctual. I should like to fix some of our impetuous English travellers in some such place as this on a day's journey. I think it would make them more satisfied with our English lines and accommodation.

It is a very similar country to Columbus—dense forest all the way. Felt rather nervous to have to take the Mississippi boat to Cairo after the disaster on Sunday evening but as it was the only route there was no alternative but to put up with it. It takes about three hours up to Cairo, which is the point of junction of the Ohio and Mississippi rivers. The river at this place is much wider than at Memphis. I should not estimate it at less than two miles. The banks all the way up are flat with pine trees growing down to the water edge, and I understand it is the same all the way down to New Orleans, which makes the journey most tedious and uninteresting.

Cairo on paper presents a grand site for a large city situate at the junction of two such rivers, with abundance of coal in the neighbourhood, but the land lies so low and is subject to the frequent inundation from the sudden rising of the rivers, which has no doubt operated against its becoming what it undoubtedly would be. It was under water when I saw it. We arrived here in about twelve hours from Memphis and did not stay longer than to get the baggage in the cars and left for Sandovah, the junction of the Ohio and Mississippi line with the Illinois Central, which we take to St. Louis.

They have sleeping cars here, but as we so soon changed I did not take one. Had to remain at Sandovah at the most miserable place possible from 2 A.M. till 5. There is no waiting room at these junctions as in England—you must take your chance and do as well as you can with dirty Americans chewing tobacco, spitting, etc. It was pitch dark when we arrived so we adjourned to the nearest place which they called an inn, and a horrid place it was. To beguile the time some of my fellow passengers took out a pack of cards and wished me to join them. I have no doubt they set me down as a proud Englishman because I would not. You meet with the queerest people in this Western country you can possibly conceive—sort of fellows you would rather see by daylight. We had the smallest dwarf with us I ever saw, with a very decent man with him taking him down to St. Louis. He was quite a man in appearance but not so high as my umbrella, as I measured him as he lay asleep in the cars.

Left Sandovah at 5 A.M. We did not get to St. Louis till 10.30, making 27½ hours from Memphis, and a most tedious journey it was. A few miles from Sandovah we get on the great Illinois prairie. It is somewhat different to what I expected. The land is in good cultivation, particularly the nearer we get to Alton, which is the opposite side of the river from St. Louis. It is most fertile land of a black colour and the wheats are looking very well. The weather is very cold at St. Louis—glad to have fires again.

April 27: St. Louis, Missouri. Found the Planters House so full that I had great difficulty in getting a room. Received here letters and newspapers from home and glad to find them well. The levee on the river here is a very busy scene; steamers as thick as they can be, ends up to the levee, loading and unloading their cargoes and passengers. We are north of cotton here, the produce seems to be tobacco, corn, flour barrels in great abundance and all descriptions of manufactured goods going down the river to the sugar plantations of Louisiana, St. Louis and the West reminds me very much of Marseilles—not in any similarity of situation or style of buildings but as a central starting point to almost any point you could name. There are booking offices here where you could take a ticket to almost any place in the United States. The different routes are posted outside on the walls as at Marseilles. I copied one for example, viz.:

St. Louis
St. Joseph
Council Bluffs
Pike's Peak
Omaha
Sioux City
Kansas
Nebraska, California
New Mexico   etc., etc.

Others to Atlantic cities by different routes—Chicago, Niagara Falls, etc.

There is an advantage in taking a through ticket in these long distances, not only a pecuniary one, but it saves much trouble as it is only necessary to check your baggage to where you stay the night, your railway ticket being available to the end of the journey. I took my ticket to Detroit by Chicago. I should have taken it to the Falls had I not wished to travel on the Great Western of Canada.

St. Louis is a most wonderful place. Although it has been the site of a town for many years up to 1830, it contained a population of less than six thousand, and previous to that was merely a trading post of the Indians, where they used to bring their buffalo skins, etc., for sale. In 1850 it contained 77,860 people and I have no doubt at the present moment it has more than double that number. (The 1860 returns will show.) It is well built, paved and watered, which is not usual in American towns. There appears to be an immense river trade but it is admirably situated in that respect on the Mississippi just below its junction with the Missouri, with all the trade of that state to back it.

April 28: This was one of the few places where I was without a letter of introduction, but knowing that one of our passengers in the *Persia,* whom we always called "Missouri" (not knowing his name) lived near St. Louis, I ascertained where he lived, and thinking that I should never have a better opportunity of seeing twenty miles of country than by driving over to see him, I went to a livery stable and engaged a horse and buggy waggon with a man to drive (who by the bye is much worse to obtain than the carriage and horse).

I set out to call upon Mr. Chambers who, I found, lived about twenty miles to the West of St. Louis at Florissant on what are called the rolling prairies in the Valley of the Missouri—in fact his place, he told me, is in the angle formed by the junction of the two rivers, not being more than twenty miles from either of them. Fortunate in meeting with him at home and very agreeably surprised at his hospitality, the more so as our acquaintance on board ship was but slight, my object in calling upon him being more for the purpose of getting out to see the style of country. He was delighted to see me and ordered out his carriage and horses and black servant (he has lots of slaves) and drove me to see their neighbourhood and system of farming. He has about 1200 acres of land in his own hands, 800 of it cleared on which he principally grows corn and grass. The timber here is not large—it appears to be a sort of second growth, the original forest being cleared; still we should call them large trees in England. The land is more in grass between this and St. Louis and being undulating ground looks more like England than what you usually see in this country. The grass grows to a great length and is very valuable for fodder, being within a reasonable distance of the St. Louis market. Mr. C tells me that he makes more of his grass than corn but unless they burn the eddish which grows a great height to destroy the insects and animalculae, the following year they are inundated with the anny worm, as it is there called, which I believe is a sort of caterpillar which destroys all vegetation before it. In fact, if once they get on the ground it is necessary to plough and cultivate the ground the following year with Indian corn and then lay it down to grass afresh, which Mr. C was then doing in a park-like field in front of his house of from sixty to seventy acres. The only way they intercept their progress is to cut deep trenches round the field. Sometimes the locust destroys the leaves of the trees in a similar manner.

Mr. Chambers gave me some seed of the honey-blade grass to take home, also some very fine specimens of Indian corn. Although it is so cold here now (28th April), it will be hot enough during the summer to ripen Indian corn. The trees are hardly budding yet and we are glad to have fires in the hotel—a great change from where I have been. Still we are in a slave state. They don't appear to me suitable for this part of the country, the climate being cold in the winter and the productions of that nature not requiring slave labour. There is also more difficulty in keeping them on the slave states bordering on the free. Mr. C has some capital horses. The pair we had in the carriage, one an entire colt, were more like first-class carriage horses than any I have seen here. The carriages are of the same peculiar light build as the buggy waggon, run easy and fast if you get on a plank road. Half the width of the road is made of planks which form a dry road in the winter and often the best in the summer, although I observe they avoid the planks when the other part of the road is fair. I suppose it draws harder crossing the planks.

After spending a most agreeable day I was obliged to bid my hospitable friends goodbye as I had arranged to leave St. Louis the following morning early, which I equally regretted with them. Mr. C was quite pressing that I should spend a week with him. I never met with more genuine hospitality in my life, but as I was a stranger to the road I had made up my mind in the morning to return by daylight as my driver knew no more of the road than I did. It was well we did so as a few miles before we got back to St. Louis he took a wrong road. Where we should have got to I can't tell but I soon found it was not the road we came by in the morning so insisted upon returning. It is not any pleasant reflection to lose one's way on those prairies after the sun goes down. We had a capital horse and got back by half past 9 to St. Louis. I was much amused with my Jehu who by the bye knew no more of the road than I did and hardly knew the way out of the city in the morning, but you can't get a Yankee ever to confess that he does not know. He will guess and calculate till he finds it out. He was a well-informed man in his way, being engaged in laying down the street railways in Boston, Mass., and had come to St. Louis for a like purpose as soon as he and his partner could get permission from the local government. He began American-like to calculate what I was; after many vain attempts he set me down at last for a Southern planter and slave holder. As I did not much like my man I thought it better to let him keep in his ignorance as they think a Southern planter a great man, but before parting I told him I was an Englishman.

I consider where I have been today in the Missouri valley the most Westerly point of my travels, being twenty or thirty miles west of St. Louis, where the time is six hours ten minutes behind London time.

April 29: Left St. Louis 7 A.M. The omnibuses cross the river on the ferry boats (as in New York) to the St. Louis, Alton and Chicago line on the Illinois side of the river. Here we saw a large escort preparing to cross the plains to California. They consist of a great number of light tilted waggons and they have to keep together in great numbers as they sometimes encounter difficulty from hostile

tribes of Indians. I believe it takes about three weeks from
St. Louis to San Francisco.

Alton. This is the roughest place for handling baggage
I ever saw. Much amused with an American whose trunk
was smashed through their rough usage, spreading all his
toggery over the platform. The English portmanteau (solid
leather) is very characteristic of the people compared with
the Yankee trunk, which looks strong and well made but
will stand no rough usage. Do what you will with the English portmanteau, it seldom hurts it. When the time is up
(and they gave this fellow precious little time to pack up
his things again) the conductor cries *All aboard*, whistles,
which is responded to by the driver's bell on the engine,
and away we start on the St. Louis, Alton and Chicago line
over the "Great Illinois Prairie." There is but little variation through this part of the state, the land being perfectly
flat and very fertile with but little wood, which only grows
in the low places or by the side of water. The land is generally settled and fenced on the sides of the railway, although for many miles you often travel over the wild open
prairie with no vestige of civilization around you but the
line of railway over which you are travelling. The great
inducement for settlers here has been the low price at which
land could be purchased, the Government having ceded to
the Railway Company (Illinois Central) 2,590,000 acres
of land as an inducement to form the line. I see by Mr.
Caird's report that more than half that quantity of land
(1,300,000) has already been sold by them to settlers at

the government price of $1¼ per acre (5/-d English), the inducement on the part of the Railway Company no doubt having been to get the line peopled through such a wild district, for although the state of Illinois contains a population of 851,470 (census 1850) it is purely a matter of accident whether there are any towns or villages near the lines of railway as they are laid out in straight lines from one large place to another. Many of the new villages where there are stations give you the idea of a child's toy shop on a large scale, as the houses are all built of wood and whitewashed and are so different to what you see in the timber country, as all the wood here has to be brought a great distance. The grass grows an enormous height even now, having had the winter snow and rain upon it. It has more the appearance of a cornfield, broken down by its own weight, than grass. You sometimes cross the wild open prairie where it is not settled, which as far as the eye can reach presents nothing but this long grass with now and then a solitary prairie hen (something between the Scotch greyhen and a duck). This open prairie resembles more the ocean on a still morning with the sun upon it, with its heavy swell without a wave, than anything I can describe. Where it is not cultivated it is often fenced and stocked with cattle in one enclosure. Near Bloomington I counted more than sixty bullocks which in England would be worth £15 to £16 each, thereby showing that the land is sometimes held in large tracts which I should think is rather the exception than the rule, although I am of opinion from observations I made that stock farming on these prairies might be profitably carried out by a man of sufficient capital and enterprise —where a man for an almost nominal sum could obtain a boundless run for his stock and on his enclosed land grow sufficient corn to feed them up in the winter. The line of railway is most rudely constructed, shaking most awfully. There is a joke here that if a man's liver is out of order let him take a trip on the Illinois Central, and if that won't cure him let him try the Chattanooga and Memphis. I can bear testimony to the shaking qualities of them, having travelled on them both. Still, roughly as these lines are made, it is a great thing to get across the State of Illinois in one day of eighteen hours from St. Louis to Chicago—281 miles. Telegraphed at Bloomington for a bed at the Tremont House, Chicago, as we should not arrive till 1 A.M. and beds were so difficult to get in St. Louis.

The trees are small, which much astonished me, seeing the fertility of the soil with the abundance of Indian corn which the land must grow. It is only surprising that they don't take better care of their stock.

Passed through Lincoln. Thought the people in some of these new Illinois villages had a more John Bull honest look about them than you often see. I attribute it to their recent arrival as settlers, not having been long enough in the country to get the Yankee beard and ways. It may only be my English prejudice but it certainly struck me so. The great want in this State to the settler is timber for fence and fuel. Although coal is abundant, time and capital will

be required to develop that. At first sight the great inducement to the newcomer to settle here is the land being all
ready to his hands. He has merely to plough and sow, after
having fenced in his allotment and built his house. Still,
on the other hand, the want of timber and the unhealthy
climate to a European for the first two or three summers
are drawbacks which a man should consider in selecting the
best place with his money in his pocket and the country before him, for when he has invested his capital the operation
of realising in hard cash is like getting butter out of a dog's
mouth.

From observations I have made I should recommend a
labouring man to settle in a forest country (undulating if
he can get it) provided he could obtain sufficient land
cleared at a fair price, with an average quantity of timber
upon it. Where there is such a vast tract of country as this
(Illinois) all flat, the want of drainage must be felt, and
the people suffer from the ague and low fevers for many
years to come.

At Bloomington we cross the Illinois Central Railway
which runs the entire length of the state from Cairo to Dun-
leith—454 miles. The best wheats I have seen in the United
States are on this line, between Sandovah and St. Louis,
rich black soil with as fine wheats as you see in England. It
is seldom you see an entire field a uniform full crop. If
there is a swamp in the field or any forest land uncleared,
there it remains, the land not being of sufficient value to
reclaim it at present. In these new states in the West the

land is set out by Government in townships six miles square —very accurately the sub-divisions being from one mile square to forty acre sections. Indian corn appears to be more generally grown than wheat—the climate is quite hot enough to ripen it. I presume the land is too rich for wheat, in fact you don't see that breadth of wheat growing you would suppose such a district would produce.

April 30: Chicago, Illinois. The Empire City of the West. Staid at the Tremont House. The city stands well on the shore of Lake Michigan, the best residences being on Michigan Avenue fronting the Lake shore. The principal street for business is Lake Street. Although it is the most rapidly improving place possible, everything now being built or recently being erected is on a very superior scale. The old wooden houses are fast giving way to more substantial structures of brick and stone, generally six storeys high. I don't know of any place that can boast of such a rapid rise (excepting perhaps the gold region in Australia). By the United States census of 1840 Chicago had a population of 4,479. The census of 1855 showed 87,000. I believe at the present time it numbers 120,000 people.

The enterprise of these people is marvellous. They have a singular system of raising the buildings in Chicago at the present time; the city being built on low land on the shore of Lake Michigan, it was found to be very deficient in drainage, consequently it was thought desirable and ordered by the local government that all the streets should be raised six feet, requiring every storekeeper to raise with soil his half of the street and lay a permanent pavement on his frontage. It has consequently left the houses six feet too low. Those houses and stores which are permanently built of stone or brick, and which it would be more expense to pull down and rebuild, are being raised in the manner described.

They place timbers under the foundations securely, then raise the whole structure by means of screws. A house at which I saw them at work had, I understood, 1,500 screws under it. One man attends to twelve screws, and he at a given signal turns each screw 1/3rd, which raises the whole building in such an imperceptible manner that there is never a crack in the walls and business is being carried on in the store at the same time. It is carried out by a company who, I understand, undertake all risk. I believe the offer to raise the Tremont House, where I am staying, is $40,000. It is no new thing, as I have myself seen many houses done, some in progress with the masons building up the brickwork under these screws, and there are many others which will either have to be pulled down or raised in like manner. Of course a whole block of buildings is raised at once. The place, particularly the street pavements, has the most uneven appearance possible, being in a transitional state. It is a very wise precaution, for although the place has risen rapidly the same causes will continue to make it grow to a monster city some day, and this may probably prevent the prevalent yellow fever with which such places are often scourged. Since the panic two years back (1857) business has been at a standstill. Previous to that for the last twelve years it has much more than doubled itself every four years. Property does not let by 2/3rds, which it did at that time.

Could not get letters at the Post Office which I had reason to think were waiting for me, but the authorities in these departments are so incompetent (the result of a democratic government where every official changes office with the change of government) and so uncivil, that when they vexed me I used to tell them that if they lived in the old country where I came from we should teach them to behave with more civility to strangers than they do here.

May 1st: Sunday. Went to the Wesleyan Methodist New Church in the morning. It is a very imposing building of white stone in a very central part of the town. The lower storey is let in shops, lawyers' offices, etc., etc. The upper one is used as a Methodist Chapel; rather a novel idea in the religious world.

Dollars and cents pervade all creation in this country. They do nothing that "won't pay," as the following anecdote which was told me will show. An Englishman passing through an American town noticed four churches and asked a Yankee on the omnibus to what denomination each belonged. "That," says he, "is a Methodist"; "And what is the next?" "Episcopalian"; the next Presbyterian; "But what is that?" says the Englishman, "it appears to be shut up." "She was a Baptist but they don't use her now, I guess she don't pay."

Met with a Canadian, Mr. Leckie, living in Michigan

Avenue, who, seeing that I was an Englishman and a stranger, very politely came up and entered into conversation. We exchanged cards and he hoped I would call upon him and the British Consul, Mr. Wilkins, in the morning, to whom he would introduce me—which I should have done had I stayed.

Went in the evening to the Second Presbyterian Church. (There are so many divisions among the different sects here that it is hard to keep pace with them, like the Presbyterians, the Second Presbyterians, the Baptists, the Hard-Shell Baptists, etc., etc.) The congregation at this church in Washington Square was small compared to the Wesleyan Church where I was in the morning. In the evening Mr. Glasson, an Englishman living here, called upon me at this hotel, seeing my name in the books as an Englishman. I was sorry my time was up at Chicago as I should have liked to have made the acquaintance of these two gentlemen, not knowing anyone in the place but a Mr. Wilson, Mr. Mitchell's friend, of whom I could make nothing. There is a great difference between the English and American character in this respect, in politeness to a stranger. The moment Mr. G saw my name on the books he called upon me and offered me every civility in his power, although I was a perfect stranger to him, but, as he observed, "We are always glad to see anyone out here from the old country." That is quite the characteristic of the Canadian people. Chicago, within the last thirty years merely a trading outpost of the West, is now one of the wonders of America, being at the present time the centre of more miles of railway than London, and can boast of houses, stores, public buildings and streets that would not disgrace that or any other city. I merely enter this to show the style of building which is not at all among the best of them, as it is an old house compared to many in the place, but the new buildings are of a very superior character.

It is most favourably situated on Lake Michigan, where I believe ships crossing the Atlantic load their cargoes without transshipment. The export trade in grain must be immense. When the prairies and wilds of Illinois and Wisconsin get better settled up, the Detroit and Milwaukee line will make a great effort by crossing the Lake at Grand Haven to get this Western traffic. They may get the passengers but it strikes me that this must be the place for the shipment of the Illinois produce and all the lower part of the State of Mississippi. It is the rich country backing these cities which makes them rise so rapidly, taking the distance. These two places, St. Louis and Chicago, are apart 281 miles, then again to Detroit 284 miles with no place of importance between them. There is no wonder that the trade should be great. You always find St. Louis and Chicago men arguing which will be the great city of the West, each of course backing their own place with great energy. There is no doubt either of them will be gigantic cities in another thirty years. The natural situation of St. Louis is the best in my opinion, on the junction of two such rivers as the Missouri and Mississippi, with such water communication to New Orleans. On the other hand, Chicago has a direct water communication through the North American lakes to the Atlantic, and when the back states get settled up the trade must be greatly increased. As a looker-on you can't but admire the energy of the people in these Western cities. Still, as a class to live among they are very different men to the Southerners. As an Englishman in Chicago observed to me, "The rakings of hell get out here. Every man for himself seems to be the order of the day."

May 2nd: Left Chicago 7 A.M. train for Detroit from the Illinois Central depot. For more than a mile the line is formed on piles in the lake, parallel with Michigan Avenue, probably two hundred yards from the shore, thereby saving a great expense in the purchase of land, and bringing two very important lines (the Illinois Central and Michigan Central) into the very heart of the place. It is low swampy land for some distance after leaving Lake Michigan. The Michigan Central Railway is the best constructed line; the trains run faster and easier than any line I have yet travelled upon in the United States. We performed the journey to Detroit—281 miles—in 10½ hours, staying to dine at Marshall. We pass through a poor country, which I should judge from appearance has been settled some time and worked out, but even here there is much forest land not cleared. The produce appears to be Indian corn and wheat, but I understand of a different sort to what they grow in the South. The timber is not large. A cord of wood is four feet high by eight feet long, four feet broad. The value of wheat in Detroit is about $3.

May 3: Detroit (Russell House—good), is a place of about 70,000 people (although the census of 1850 gives but 21,019). These places rise so rapidly in ten years that you hardly know whether the people are telling you the correct population. It is a well-built place with one very wide street parallel with the river, laid out on the American plan of building cities, and has a considerable frontage on the river. As two people from our own village had settled out here and from the address I had given me I ascertained that they lived within thirty miles of this place, I was anxious to see them. Left Detroit on the Milwaukee line for Birmingham, a small station twenty miles off, near to East Bloomington, where I had hoped to find them. They only this spring removed further up in the country. After great difficulty in obtaining a carriage and horses, with which the man declared it was impossible to reach their place (a distance of eight miles) and return within three hours, which was the time the next train passed, and after considerable parley with the man, we risked it and set off on the most awful roads, and after driving three quarters of an hour came up to Cooper Pickering's place, for I think the fellow did his best to get me there when I told him I should like to see them and I must get into Canada that night. That was the only train I could get on by. I found him in possession of eighty acres of land, which he has recently purchased—10 acres in wheat, 20 acres Indian corn,

10 acres oats, 5 acres potatoes, the rest wood and water. He has one yoke of oxen and 3 horses, 40 sheep, wife and 3 children, who look healthy—2 boys and 1 girl, the eldest 5 years old. I copied all this down as fast as they told it me, knowing that her mother, Mrs. Turner, would be anxious to know what amount of worldly goods they possessed.

Mrs. Pickering was very glad to see me, from Halton, her native place, but had not the remotest idea who I was till I told her. She complains so terribly of the ague, which is the great scourge of all these new countries to newcomers. The summers are so hot, they have no spring. The trees now (May 3rd) are quite dead, not a vestige of anything green to be seen. Still, Pickering tells me their harvest will be ready before ours in England. It is hot enough to ripen Indian corn. He has a sister living within a mile. They have 40 acres of land. This woman knew me better than her sister and asked after many Halton people. She has been out here seven years, has three children. They do not look so healthy as her sister's although the place they live in is higher ground. They all complain of the ague. As they had neither of them heard from their mother since their arrival in this country, I promised to take their address and request their friends in England to communicate with them as soon as I returned.

Joseph Pickering,
Franklin Post Office,
Oaklands County,
Michigan, U.S.

This one seemed much better satisfied with her lot in this country than her sister. Although it would afford them great pleasure to see anyone from the old country and particularly from the place of their birth, and I was glad to have seen the position of such settlers in the far West, still there is rather a melancholy feeling in calling to see people who have renounced the country of their birth, and found the new one not exactly that land of plenty that they expected. I look upon it as a sort of voluntary transportation. A man wants to be badly off indeed in the old country to better himself here as a tiller of the soil; not but what he can get plenty of the necessaries of life, but many comforts which he values but lightly in England he is totally destitute of here, but to a woman it is seven times worse.

Undoubtedly their children, bred and born there and knowing nothing better than a squatter's life, will, as population increases and land improves in value, be much better off than they would have been in England, their parents being agricultural labourers. But the condition of the man and woman emigrating and obtaining possession of 80 to 100 acres of land in the United States is but little removed from that of a labouring man in England, minus many comforts obtainable in a civilized country. In fact, I should prefer the condition of the well-employed English labourer on some of our large farms to the average of these new settlers; at the same time, if the rate of wages in England be low and work difficult to obtain, I would recommend any industrious man to go. But the selection of a good situation favourably situate for railways or water communication (in fact the latter being the only means of transport previous to railways) has been so much more sought after that you usually find it well settled up near the large rivers.

A healthy situation naturally well drained with a fair amount of timber on the land are all-important considerations which are too often lost sight of by such people. As any of the land in the West is to be bought at a low price compared to an Englishman's ideas and as it will all undoubtedly increase in value as it becomes settled up, of course there will be a greater increase in the more favourable localities.

The price of beef here is 8 cents per lb. by the piece. $6 the cwt.; wheat $1½ the bushel; corn 75 cents to $1 the bushel; oats 50 cents the bushel. The usual produce is 20 bushels of wheat per acre, 50 bushels of corn, 40 bushels oats.

The livers of animals here are generally diseased, which proves the unhealthiness of the climate, and all the people have a sallow complexion, which is easily accounted for by the sudden transition from a Canadian winter to heat that will ripen Indian corn. The man who drove me to Pickering's was a very intelligent man and was quite pleased when he found the object of my visit, and was equally anxious with me that they should hear from their mother in England, and promised me when I left that if a letter was sent according to that direction he would see it safely delivered as he was the postmaster of the district, whose business it is to meet the trains from Detroit daily.

Sorry that my time was so limited but if I did not leave Birmingham at 11 I could not get into Canada that night, as I had previously arranged to be in Guelph the following day.

Returned to the Russell House, Detroit, and spent the day in exploring the lions of the place till 7.30, when the train leaves on the Canadian side for Hamilton. The opposite side of the river from Detroit is Windsor. Our baggage is just looked at but they are not very particular in the examination—at all events I found them so.

Got to London about half past 11, where I staid the night at the Tecumsa House in preference to travelling all night, as I found I could by an early train get to Guelph in good time.

Tecumsa House very good. What they built such a large hotel for in such a place I can't conceive, for this London consists of a few detached wooden whitewashed houses, rather a burlesque on the old city whose name it bears.

May 4th: Up at 5 o'clock to breakfast and catch the first train to Guelph. Although the time for bed was short it is far better than travelling all night, particularly when you can stay at a clean hotel like this. At the Harrisburg junction we leave the main line and take a short branch to Guelph, although my best way was to have taken the branch of the Grand Trunk from London to Guelph direct, but being somewhat interested in the Great Western I was anxious to see the mode of construction, stations, general appearance of the line and its management. Although trade is bad at the present time, through a succession of bad harvests in the province, consequently the dividends are small, the line contrasts very favourably with the American lines in durability, construction and general management.

On the Canadian lines there are two classes, 1st and 2nd. Still these people do not travel in the same manner as their neighbours do in the United States. There does not appear to be that pushing go-aheadism you see in the United States. On the other hand, you never see any tobacco chewing, but the people have a clean orderly look, quite different from the Yankees.

Weighed at Harrisburg 152 lbs.

Having a letter to a Mr. Stone at Guelph, who I understood was an extensive farmer, I was anxious to see the style of farming in that part of Western Canada. He breeds shorthorn cattle and Cotswold sheep in a very enterprising manner, having spared no expense in importing the best blood from England for that purpose. His shorthorns would do credit to any herd in England, although I should fear they are too good and expensive for such a country as Canada West, where their principal herbage is among the woods more suitable for small hardy cattle. I should have a better opinion of the first cross between the first-class shorthorn and the beasts of the country, where you would not lose the hardiness of the little beasts and at the same time increase their feeding properties.

He has some very good Cotswold ewes and rams, and Berkshire pigs. I sincerely hope it may answer his purpose as he is a most enterprising man and very sanguine of success. He speaks favourably of the sales he has had of his shorthorns but I should fear the country is not sufficiently wealthy as yet to give him prices that would remunerate him for such an outlay. Beasts may succeed but sheep can never be kept in large numbers in such a climate, where it is necessary to house them and their food from October till this (May 4th), or even later. They grow capital Swede turnips which are all stored in houses covered on immense thicknesses with straw and manure. The wool on these housed sheep does not grow natural as in the open air. The farm I saw was famous land, growing as good turnips and seeds as our best wolds, and, save the climate, as suitable for profitable sheep farming.

On all these farms there is a deal of forest, which, as the timber gets cleared, comes under cultivation. Saw some which he called cleared and which he intends breaking up next week for oats on which the stumps of trees are standing much thicker than we should have any idea of ploughing amongst. He has no fear of a good crop which, sown in another week (May 11th), will be ripe before our harvest in England. He has another farm on the opposite side of the road which I had not time to visit, on which he keeps Southdown sheep. I should think them much better suited to this country than the long-wooled sheep, as they bear housing and live where the long wools will not. True,

the same difficulty applies to their food. It was Guelph
Spring Fair for horses and beasts. They bring their beasts
to market very poor. I am much surprised they don't take
better care of them during the winter as it is a fine country for roots and fodder might easily be obtained in the
summer.

Met a man at an inn here who knew North Lincolnshire
and Yorkshire—a brother of Mr. Jackson's Riston. It is
a very pretty undulating country around here and Galt,
and I understand as well farmed as any part of Canada
West.

Quite pleased on my return to Guelph from Mr. Stone's
farm to see the British flag flying, after seeing nothing but
Stars and Stripes so long. The Canadians in this part are
very loyal and wonderfully attached to the old country.
The Queen's birthday, 24th May, is observed throughout
the province as a general holiday. I should like some of our
countrymen to come into Canada and hear these people
speak of the old country. They little prize the advantages
under which they live but let them come out here, they
would think more highly of them. After a very agreeable
and instructive day with Mr. Stone and dining at the table
d'hote of the British American Hotel, left Guelph by the
4 P.M. train for Hamilton and arrived at 7. Staid at the
American Hotel—I believe the best in the place, but not
good.

Englishmen keep up their nationality, whether at home
or abroad. We had no sooner got in the cars leaving Guelph

than the influence of Guelph beer began to show itself upon one of our passengers, who had been fighting at the fair. It struck me as so characteristic of our people, always getting drunk at a fair.

May 5th: Hamilton. A small town with one main street through it, situated very pleasantly at the foot of the mountain (as it is called). Met at the British American Hotel, to my great surprise, Mr. Urquhart, Montreal, who had just returned from England. He very kindly renewed his invitation to me to visit him at Montreal. Immediately after breakfast I called upon Mr. Reynolds, Director of the Great Western Railway of Canada. As he and a party of the directors were that day going to Buffalo to inspect some new steamers building there for connecting the traffic on Lake Michigan between Grand Haven and Milwaukee, he very kindly asked me to accompany them as his guest and spend the day. I could not refuse so kind an offer although my time was somewhat limited, so returned quickly to the hotel where I had only just time to pack up my things, pay my bill and get down to the station, which is a mile from the town.

The Directors met us at the station, to whom I was introduced by Mr. R. They have a beautiful car for their own use, fitted up with every convenience, in which we travelled as far as Suspension Bridge, where their line ends. We here obtain the first view of the falls of Niagara, about 1½ miles distant. We passed over the Desjardins Canal, where such a fearful accident happened some two or three years back by the giving way of the bridge. It is a deep ravine over which there is now a substantial bridge, the former one being merely trestlework.

This Canal is the connecting link between the two lakes (Erie and Ontario), without which the falls of Niagara would present an obstacle to the navigation of this chain of North American lakes.

Suspension Bridge, Niagara Falls: As I was to return again in the evening Mr. Reynolds very kindly sent Mr. Price, the station master, to secure a room for me at the Monteagh Hotel, on the American side, as the Clifton House was not yet open for the season.

Arrived at Buffalo about 2 P.M., where carriages were in readiness to take us to the docks and shipbuilding yards, where these steamers—the *Detroit* and *Milwaukee*—are in course of construction. They appear to be very superior boats of the kind and fitted up with every convenience to make them desirable. I find the largest timber for this purpose is brought from Florida. They anticipate crossing Lake Michigan from Grand Haven to Milwaukee in six hours in these boats. Went through the various stores where all the interior fittings are being prepared. All the bedding, curtains, towels, etc., etc., are sewn by machinery. Never saw a sewing machine at work before and was much surprised to see how quickly and with what precision the work is done. After inspecting the boats and other work in connection with them, we drove round the town of Buffalo, which is a well-built, thriving place. I don't admire the style of architecture—the houses have a heavy look, not built with that taste you often see. It reminds you of a well-to-do place retired from trade.

Returned to the hotel, where a very sumptuous dinner awaited us, and got back to Niagara by 9 o'clock, where I parted with my friends. Much pleased with Mr. Bridges, the Managing Director, whom I found a very intelligent man. Surprised on taking up the Buffalo paper the following morning to find the paragraph below. I was not aware we were such great people, but it is not often you find a Yankee lose an opportunity of puffing himself off.

VISITORS TO THE NEW BOATS—The new boats that are being built at the yard of Messrs. Bidwell & Mason, under the supervision of Julius Movius, Esq., for the Detroit and Milwaukee Railroad Company, were visited and inspected on Thursday, by a large party of gentlemen from abroad, mostly composed of Railroad magnates interested in the line. Among them were the following well-known gentlemen:

Mr. Brydges, Managing Director, G.W.R. and President Detroit & Milwaukee.
Mr. Reynolds, Financial Director, G.W.R. and V.P. Detroit and Milwaukee.
Mr. Inron, Director, G.W.R.
Mr. Beecher, Director, G.W.R.
Mr. Park, Manager, Com. Bk. of Canada
Mr. Vessey, of England
Hon. E. Corning, Pres. N.Y.C.R.R.
Hon. Dean Richmond, V.P., N.Y.C.R.R.

Hon. Mr. Banker, Chief Clerk, N.Y.C.R.R.
Hon. Briggs, Freight Manager, Hud. R.R.R.

After a thorough examination of the two splendid vessels, the visitors one and all expressed their admiration in the highest terms, and complimented both builder and superintendent upon having produced as fine specimens of naval architecture as ever floated. Such compliments from such men are not idle ones nor valueless.

May 6th: Niagara Falls. As the Clifton House was not yet open for the season I staid at the Monteagh Hotel, Suspension Bridge, where Mr. Price had ordered me a room, and met me with letters posted for the Clifton House. As we were nearly two miles from the Falls I was up early and took a carriage on the American side to Goat Island, which is a beautiful island of probably 100 acres studded with fine timber and laid out in drives and pleasure grounds dividing the American from the Canadian or Great Horse Shoe Fall. You cross from the mainland over the rapids by a succession of bridges, after paying a small toll. This island is private property and I am told the income arising from these tolls during the season is something enormous. The rapids are very beautiful and would be a lion in themselves were they not in the immediate vicinity of one so much larger. Although the Falls of Niagara, as everyone knows, are formed by the discharge of the waters of Lake Erie into Lake Ontario, the two lakes are many miles apart, consequently the waters narrow into a river for some miles back from the Falls, and these rapids are the first breaking of the waters over the rocks for perhaps more than a mile before they get to the great fall. Goat Island divides the great body of water—that on the right hand forming the Great Horse Shoe Fall on the Canadian side, with the American on the left. The waters of these rapids present one mass of foam breaking over the rocks before they come to the great fall. The body of water forming the American fall is perhaps not more than 1/3rd of the Canadian, still I think it is quite as beautiful, pouring over in one unbroken torrent, and on that account appears to fall a greater height.

A short walk on the Island brings you in view of the great Canadian fall. This is certainly one of the greatest wonders in creation, unequalled in grandeur. I would say to those who have the time and opportunity, "Go and see it," as no description can give you any adequate idea of the grandeur of it. A small footbridge from the Island brings you to a tower built on the very edge of the rock of the Horse Shoe Fall. The view from the summit of this tower is fearfully grand with the immense body of water on each side of you pouring down into the abyss below and you standing as it were on the very edge, where but one false step might be fatal. The contemplation of the view around you standing on this spot does inspire a feeling of solemnity, which can only be appreciated by those who have witnessed it. What an extraordinary impression it must have produced upon the mind of the first white man who discovered this stupendous cataract among the wilds of the

Indians before any civilisation had penetrated these forests. What a wonderful change since then! Now there is quite a small town on the American side and many large hotels, caused no doubt by the great annual influx of visitors. We are also within view of a great engineering work—the Niagara Suspension Bridge, which is a most elegant structure, 820 feet span from tower to tower, with an elevation of 258 feet above the river.

It was built by an independent company but now used by the Great Western of Canada and New York Central Railroads, the upper road being used for the railroad lines and the lower one for carriages and foot passengers. I walked upon it while the train passed over us. I understand the Company receive from the Great Western of Canada $45,000 annually for the privilege of running their trains over the bridge.

After spending some time on the Island, I drove back through the village of Niagara, where you are besieged by people keeping stores of Indian work for sale. Bought many things at the Six Nation Indian store, where they keep Indian women working the fans and beadwork, etc., which they do in a very beautiful manner. Crossed the Suspension Bridge (the charge for crossing which is 50 cents for a carriage and 25 cents each person) but through the kindness of my friend, Mr. Reynolds, I had a free pass during my stay. The view of the Falls from this, the Canadian side, is most beautiful as it embraces a view of the whole.

Mr. Vessey of England

The Clifton House Hotel must be a delightful place to stay during the season, commanding a view of both falls, but I should think very damp from the spray constantly arising from the falls. But of all the lovely places to erect a mansion is the adjoining property on the slope of the hill well backed by timber and commanding a full view of the falls and surrounding scenery, but sufficiently removed from the water to be beyond the influence of the damp. It was the property of the late Mr. Zimmerman, an influential man in that part in railways, etc., who was about erecting a mansion, having built offices, cottages, gardens, laid out the grounds, lighted the place with gas, etc., etc., and laid the foundation of his house, which he never lived to see further than it at present exists. He was killed in a railway accident and lies buried in his own grounds. It is not an uncommon thing in America for people to be buried in their own lands.

Drove to the Burning Spring, which is singular. The water is bubbling up in a well and when you put a light to it, it throws out a very powerful flame. I believe pipes were laid on to convey the gas to the adjoining house but it did not succeed. I suppose it was not sufficiently pure although the light appears strong.

On our return saw some runaway niggers fighting. There are many about here. They have a settlement at Chatham but they are a bad disorderly lot. The magistrates here tell me there is more crime committed by them than any other class, which I can readily believe. They are a people not

139

capable of self-government, and although they are here in a land of freedom a Canadian winter is not suited to their constitution.

In the afternoon I drove to the Indian Settlement, about six miles from Niagara, expecting to find them dressed in costume and living in wigwams. Although I was disappointed to find them living in wooden houses and most of them cultivating land, as the man who drove me observed, I should perhaps have been more so if I had gone away without seeing them, although they did not come up to my expectations of Indian life. They are a dirty vagabond lot, not unlike our gipsies, preferring anything rather than cultivating the soil. The chief dresses like other people and speaks English, which many of the others can do, but if a stranger goes they pretend they cannot, particularly the women. I think the dodge of this is they set a price upon their work, in which they are remarkably clever, in fans, beadwork, etc., and pretend that they don't understand you, particularly if you offer them any less than the price they have fixed. Finding them at work I bought some of the things, knowing that I could better rely upon it as the genuine Indian work having seen them work it myself, than what I should get at the stores. The chief told me the original settlement was 1,920 acres, since which 4,339 acres have been purchased by the government and ceded to them, making together 6,259 acres. The present population is 316 and about 60 families. When any of them marry and want a piece of land to settle upon, the chief sets it out for them at his discretion, generally about nine acres according to the family, but as I have before observed they did not make good citizens. A roving life, hunting, shooting, fishing, is more congenial to their taste than settling down to till the soil. They have a church on this settlement. Sunday is decidedly the best day for visiting the settlement as the people are all at home and dressed more in costume on that day than another. The women wear short gowns and long petticoats. We saw many of them as we returned. Lost our way, and for about an hour were driving among those backwoods not at all to my satisfaction. It is not a pleasant idea to lose one's way with night coming on in such a country and among such people. Very glad, after a circuitous route, to find the road we came by and get safely back to the Monteagh Hotel, which is in a more civilized country.

Excepting in the bronzed colour and flat features and meeting with them on the Indian Settlement, there is no characteristic to distinguish them from the people around them. The Red Indian of old is fast disappearing before the white man. I believe they do not much exceed 300,000 on the whole American continent at the present time and they are gradually receding with the setting sun to Kansas, Nebraska, New Mexico, Oregon, and such remote regions beyond the Mississippi, where they and the buffalo have still undisputed possession. I believe there are occasionally hostile tribes who attack the caravans in crossing the plains to California by the overland route. There are those now living who had to defend their homes from the Red Indian, where populous cities now stand. How long they will continue as a people is not for us to say, but my impression is that whoever lives to see another half century over will find the pure blood Red Indian and the buffalo among the things that have been. I was very sorry when at Memphis in the West to find that a tribe from Arkansas had been in the city only a few days previous, as I should have very much liked to have seen them, as they are so much more in their aboriginal state than those we meet with on the Settlements.

May 7: As the train for Toronto did not leave till 10.20 I drove again to the Falls to take a farewell view and only regretted time did not admit of my remaining longer. I think the more you see of the Falls the more grand they appear.

I found the Monteagh House very clean and comfortable. The only objection, it is so far from the Falls, and cabmen are not low in their charges. It is well to make your own bargain and not take a carriage from the hotel, which I did, to my cost. The only satisfaction in such a course is that you are an Englishman and it is what all Britons do.

As we cross Suspension Bridge all baggage is examined, being the frontier into Canada. They give you but little trouble on that score unless they think you don't look honest. Much amused with the custom house officers and a black man in the cars, who was evidently smuggling some shoes, on which I believe there is a heavy duty in Canada.

Called upon Mr. Reynolds in passing through Hamilton, where we stay half an hour. Left him the *Stamford Mercury*, with which he was much amused, as it contained much Lincolnshire news. There is little variation in the country. It is well settled and cultivated up to Toronto, as the line runs near the Lake, which of course would be the first land cleared and cultivated, offering as it does greater facilities for getting away the timber.

Toronto: Rossin House. The only decent inn in the province. Called upon Mr. Harrington, a gentleman I accidentally met in a railway carriage just before leaving England. He was very kind and invited me to his house to dine with him and in the evening drove me round the place in his carriage and showed me where he was going to erect a house for himself. There are some Government grounds laid out as a public park extending $1\frac{1}{2}$ miles and well planted, through which is a very pleasant drive. At the upper end is a large college in course of erection, which is intended as a university for the province. It is built with funds arising from lands set out for educational purposes which have now become valuable. Toronto much resembles an English town, the streets are straight but not crossed in the block fashion so common in America, which is a great drawback in every way, particularly in a sanitary point of view. Any stranger who has ever travelled in America must be struck with the great facility there is in finding his way in a city laid out on the block principle, compared with the old-fashioned cities of Europe.

The Americans are certainly far ahead of us in building

cities. It may be said it was a new country and they had the advantage of laying it out on a uniform plan, but what have these Canadians been about?

Toronto is a neat, well-built place with one principal street but there is no mistaking the fact that there is not that pushing enterprise among the people you see in the States. On the other hand the people are as great a contrast. They look so clean, respectable and well dressed. Those democratic bears are not so common here. The Governor General's house, Government Offices and Houses of Parliament are of a very unpretending character. I was quite disappointed in them, expecting something on a much grander scale, being the alternate seat of Government for the United Provinces. They are hardly equal to the Court House in a provincial town in England. The railway runs into the town by the lake shore.

The two lines—Grank Trunk and Great Western of Canada—meet here and have a joint station. The only case of incivility I met with in my travels was at this place. I applied at the Commercial Bank of the Midland District to get a circular note cashed and was about a quarter of an hour beyond the usual time, not being aware of the hours of business among banks in the province (they close at 3 o'clock), but as it was of importance to me to get some money that afternoon as I left early on the Monday morning, I apologised to the cashier (who had plenty of money on the counter) and asked him if he would be good enough to cash me the note, explaining the circumstances, but he was one of those methodistical gentlemen who never transgress rules. After a short parley and finding him inexorable, I thought it my duty not to leave him without giving him a bit of my mind, as they say. I told him I thought he was a disgrace to the country to which he belonged, as I had travelled many thousands of miles and had never met with the same incivility. If I had met with such treatment from a Yankee I should not have been surprised, but from my own countryman in a distant province I must confess I did feel amazed. He would have changed the money before I left, but Englishman-like I would be under no obligation, so slammed the door and walked off. If I had known a director of that bank, as I did of the other one, I should have shown that fellow up, as I never find those methodistical fellows over honest.

I afterwards went to the Branch Bank of Montreal, notwithstanding which I was later still. They cashed my note without a remark, although their hours were the same.

Exchange 72:63 per £15 English.

May 8th: Sunday. Went to the Episcopal Church with Mr. Harrington. Very superior singing and music but not unlike many English churches; wanting in that apparent devotion you see in the Presbyterian Churches in the Southern States where the congregation *sing* and the *Minister preaches*. On leaving church, met with Mr. Betley, one of our passengers in the *Persia*. Dine at 2 at the Rossin House on Sundays. There is often a great swell on these

Lakes. Lake Ontario is very rough. This afternoon it is very cold here—hedges and trees are just budding.

May 9: Left Toronto early for Kingston (170 miles) on the Grand Trunk Railway. Very cold—we had fires in the cars. What a cold, cheerless country this appears after the forward vegetation of the Southern States! It has been gradually colder every day since I left Georgia. We are now on the Great Trunk Railway of Canada, upwards of eight hundred miles in its entire length. It is equally well formed with the Great Western, which certainly contrasts very favourably with the United States railroads. They never call them railways here. The line runs for many miles on the lake shore and I should judge very inexpensive in its construction. Arrived at Kingston at 2 P.M. Met young Worsley, who was delighted to see me. Asked him to dine with me at the British American Hotel at 5 o'clock and drove up to the town which is two miles from the station. It is an old-fashioned inn—English style—quite a contrast to what I have lately met with. The town of Kingston is wonderfully Irish in appearance. If I had been set down here not knowing what part of the world I was in, I should immediately have said it was a small town on the western coast of Ireland. It reminded me of Spilsby in one respect, being indebted to crime and poverty for its only building of importance. There is a good Court House just erected of the blue stone of the district. I attended the Assizes which were going on at the time.

May 10th: Left Kingston (by the Toronto and Montreal boat) at 6 A.M. for Prescott, as everyone said I must see the Lake of the Thousand Islands, with which I was much disappointed. The scenery is pretty, but nothing grand like many other places. It has its beauties and is made more of than it deserves. I perhaps did not see it to advantage as the weather was so cold and there was no foliage on the trees. Although the boats are very clean and comfortable, I would recommend anyone to take the rail in preference, which I did, to Montreal, avoiding the rapids of the St. Lawrence.

Arrived at Prescott at 11 and found Can Brackenbury quite well and living very comfortably. He is married and has three children. Staid that day and the following till 5 P.M. with him. He introduced me to a Mr. Ellis, who is a leading man there and carrying on an extensive brewery, which is rather a novel thing as ale is not drunk to that extent here as in England. As the people are more English around here I hope it may succeed. In the United States you get nothing but the lager beer which is a sort of German beer of an inferior kind. In the afternoon Mr. Ellis met us and we crossed the St. Lawrence to Ogdensburg on the American side.

It is called a village but it numbers about seven thousand people. So much for American enterprise. Here we have all life and activity. Houses rising in all directions and everything on the move. What a contrast from poor Prescott on the Canadian side, barely struggling for an existence.

147

Left Prescott at 5 P.M. May 11th and arrived at Montreal at 10 P.M. After spending two very pleasant days with Can I dare say he was equally pleased to talk over English news with me. The place where he lives, Prescott, stands on the side of a hill well above the river and I should take it to be very healthy. He showed me some gloves made of a young bear he had shot. There is a short line of railway to Ottawa, fifty-four miles, which is to be the future seat of Government for the Upper and Lower Provinces United, which no doubt will eventually have a beneficial effect upon Prescott.

May 12: Montreal. Donagano's Hotel. Very unwell. Staid in the house till 12. Received letters and newspapers. Found the *North Briton* would sail from Quebec on the 14th. Wrote home to catch that mail. Called upon Mr. Urquhart in the afternoon. He entered my name at the news room which gave me access to see the news whenever I pleased during my stay.

Disastrous news from Europe. War. War Consols 88 and everything else in proportion. Went with him to see the great Victoria Bridge now building over the St. Lawrence—a span of two miles. This is among the greatest engineering wonders of the age. I presume the ice in the winter and the rapid current are the great difficulties with which they have had to contend. It is a tubular bridge on piers of solid masonry to resist the ice (twenty-five in number) and I am told every pier contains more stone than the great Cathedral Church in Montreal. I walked in the tube as far as it was completed and then on the top. There is one tube in the centre standing by itself, which was built on the ice during the last winter and completed so that it rested on each pillar before the ice gave way. I have no doubt it would save the company an immense sum as it obviates the necessity of all the trestlework within which the men stand to form the tube, which is made of continuous sheets of iron rivetted together. I only regretted after I left, and very nearly returned from Quebec for the purpose of driving in one of those rivets (which I have no doubt the men would have allowed me to do for a trifle), thereby taking part in the greatest engineering work on that side of the Atlantic.

The workmen employed in the bridge live in the Irish Settlement which consists of a number of wooden houses erected by the people of Montreal at the time of the great Irish exodus, when they came over in such numbers and died at the rate of 150 to 200 a day in the city, that it was thought so injurious to the health of the city that this place was built for their reception.

The tubular bridge over the Menai Straits is 1,513 feet with two spans of 482 feet each and two of 175 feet. It has two million rivets and the weight of iron is twenty thousand tons. This seems a gigantic undertaking, but compared with the Victoria bridge on the St. Lawrence, a span of two miles, it looks small.

May 13: Spent the morning in taking a general view of the town, shipping, markets, etc., etc. Went over the *North*

Briton. The Canadian steamers are very fine vessels. I should not have objected to return by one of them from Quebec had I not made arrangements to visit New York again and return in the *Persia*. Went to the news room where we see the English papers. Worse news every day. General preparation for war. Many failures reported on the Stock Exchange.

There is a monument in honor of Nelson in Notre Dame Street, which the Americans would call "a very dilapidated party." It certainly is a disgrace to the city that it should be kept in such a state. They should either pull it down or keep it as it deserves to be, but I take it this place is full of Catholics and French.

Called upon Mr. Pickering (Woolley's friend), fixed to lunch with him at his club at half past 1 o'clock. Met there a gentleman who was to return in the *North Briton* who had been making a tour of the United States like myself.

Met Mr. Urquhart at 4 by appointment and drove up the mountain as far as the waterworks, where we obtain a good view of the city below and the St. Lawrence. It is a noble river here. The trade has hardly commenced yet although the river is clear of ice. The winds have been unfavourable, which has kept the ships back. Of course when trade does begin the quay presents a very busy scene, as it is the great depot for all the Canadian trade, and as all business must be done between May and October it causes great activity during that time.

May 14: Left Montreal at 7 A.M. for Quebec. We go down the river a mile before we cross the St. Lawrence to the railway on the other side, having in view the Victoria Bridge in the distance. This will soon be done away with as it is contemplated to open the bridge in October. For some distance the country is cleared and settled but has a peculiar look, being inhabited by the French Canadians, who share their lands among all their children, which in time has the effect of dividing it into the most minute shreds. The country then becomes wild and barren, covered with timber but of inferior growth. I have seen no large timber since I came into Canada, such as you see in passing through Georgia and some of the Southern States, but that may be accounted for as the lines of railway often run in low places near rivers or lakes where the communication has been more easy to get their timber away by water carriage, consequently the original forest has been cleared for many years. I understand the finest timber in Quebec is brought down the Ottawa, a distance of eight hundred miles.

At Richmond, which is the junction with the Portland line, we stay to lunch. The country is very monotonous and uninteresting the whole way to Point Levis. The opposite side of the St. Lawrence to Quebec where we leave the cars and take the steamer over to the other side, a few miles from Point Levis, we pass the Chaudière Falls and obtain a fine view of the City of Quebec with its citadel on the summit of the rock overhanging the lower part of the town.

Quebec: Arrived here about 5 P.M. and immediately proceeded to the Russell House. Dirty, ill-ventilated and small, like all the Canadian Hotels excepting the Rossin House in Toronto. I don't think there is a good hotel in Upper or Lower Canada. After dinner took a caleche, which is *the* carriage of Quebec, a sort of old-fashioned chaise on two wheels with a top to it, and called upon R. B. Dobell, Esq. (Messrs. G. B. Symes & Co.), one of our passengers in the *Persia*, who very kindly asked me when I visited Quebec that I would come to see him. We went up to the Citadel that evening, which is very extensive and appears as strongly fortified as it is possible to be. It is the Gibraltar of this country. We had but little difficulty in getting admission as he knows many of the officers. The view from the summit is very beautiful, embracing an area of many miles with the mountains in the distance and the St. Lawrence below. It reminded me more of the Italian scenery around Lake Lugano than anything I can describe.

May 15: Sunday. Accompanied Mr. Dobell to the Episcopal Church; the same in the afternoon. Met there Mr. Forsyth to whom I had a letter of introduction. He asked me to dine with him tomorrow at his country residence, Cap Rouge, up the river six or seven miles. Dined with Mr. Dobell at his rooms, No. 3 Mount Caunel, in the upper town where there is an open terrace overhanging the river, from which is a magnificent view of the surrounding country, with the river and shipping below. It is the public promenade of Quebec in an evening.

In the evening we took a walk on the heights over the plains of Abraham, where Gen. Wolfe fell. There is a small monument to his memory to denote the spot. Found plenty of ice in the back streets (May 15th), the remnant of their severe winters. Of course in the great thoroughfares in the City, particularly in the lower town, it has been cleared away. At the hotels you see large blocks brought in for daily use. I saw a man breaking up one of these huge blocks one day, which I should think was three feet square. On payment of a very small rate for the season a sufficient quantity is brought to every house in Montreal and Quebec for their daily use.

May 16: Called upon Mr. Forsyth Snr. Mr. Dobell very kindly introduced me at the news room, which is always a great advantage to a stranger in a foreign place. After transacting some business—he is engaged in the lumber trade—we took a carriage together to the Falls of Montmorency, a distance of seven miles from Quebec. The country around here is chiefly occupied by the French Canadians, a sad, indolent people. Their houses are very clean.

Falls of Montmorency. The body of water is not great but as it falls such a great height it is very beautiful as it all appears to rise again as spray. A short distance from the Falls through fields you come to the natural steps which explain their meaning, the rocks being shelved in the form of steps. Here we found plenty of ice and snow, and having with me some brandy I proposed to Mr. Dobell that it would be the correct thing as became true Britons to drink the health of her most gracious Majesty, particularly as I was in the most northernly part of her dominions I had ever been.

It was a beautiful day, although in mixing the brandy with the ice it froze the particles of ice and snow round the cup as hard as possible. I suppose the contact of the spirit with the intense cold would have that effect.

At the entrance to the Falls of Montmorency you meet with people selling the Indian work, there being an Indian village at the Falls of Lorette (which we had intended driving over to see, but I was not very anxious as I had seen similar ones before). We returned after a most agreeable drive to Quebec. At the news room found a telegram from England with better news. Funds go. Less probability of England being engaged in war. In the evening drove to Cap Rouge to dine with Mr. Forsyth, Jnr. The scenery on the St. Lawrence is very beautiful; the banks being considerably elevated just above his house he gets a beautiful view of the river, with the rafts constantly floating down. Some of them are an immense size covering many acres. The bulk of the largest timber you see at Quebec is brought down the Ottawa, a distance of 700 or 800 miles. I can't at this moment recollect the name of these large rafts but they are composed of a number of small ones slung together, each of which occupies about a quarter of an acre. They get the best buffalo skins from the Ottawa. The Hudson Bay company having the monopoly of the trade, Montreal is the great depot for the sale of them. I understand thousands of them are killed annually by the Indians, merely for the hide and tongue, leaving the carcasses to rot on the plains.

It is a very interesting sight to notice one of these rafts coming down the river. They are most systematically made, having to travel so far before they get to Quebec. Some of the larger ones have many wooden houses upon them, in which the people live who navigate them. They always sell the entire raft in one lot to some of the large merchants, break up their houses and go back to the forests on the Ottawa to work out another for the following year.

Spent a very agreeable evening at Mr. Forsyth's. Every available space seems to be taken up on the river as a timber dock between this place and Quebec. As in the Southern States of America, cotton is *the* article, so is timber at Quebec.

May 17: Mr. Dobell, who is very extensively engaged in the lumber trade, very kindly took me over many of the large timber yards, Messrs. S. B. Symes & Co., Messrs. Gilmour, etc., etc. Yards they can hardly be called, as they are not on land. They chiefly lie floating in the river on what are called booms, which is a space enclosed with floating pieces of timber rising and falling with the tide to prevent the pieces within those booms floating away. The divisions between each boom are the only firm places to walk upon; to see the timber in the booms you have to jump from piece to piece and be careful you don't slip into the St. Lawrence. These booms extend some miles up the river —I think we drove more than three miles, timber all the way, and they extend much higher up the river. The piles of timber which they land on the shore above the influence of the tide they call mulnettes. Saw them loading two ships with timber for Europe for Mr. Dobell. I see there is great art in stowing it away, neither to lose space nor cut the long pieces, which of course deteriorate their value. They fill up the intermediate spaces with stave loads and loads of which you see lying on the quays here. Timber at Quebec reminds you of the colliery district where every man has a load of coals shot down at his door, not caring to have a house to take care of them. Took a caleche, the peculiar carriage of Quebec, on two wheels with a top to it which was very useful this morning as it was a-pouring rain. They are the most uneasy conveyances you ever rode in. Lunched at the hotel as Mr. D was obliged to forego his engagement to dine with me as his friend, Mr. Symes, had only that day returned from Europe, who he was very anxious to see.

Accounts from England better. Funds firmer. Rainy day. Inspected some buffalo robes and white bear skins. Bought views of Quebec and music recommended by Mr. D. The upper town of Quebec is a delightful place to live in—so high and healthy. The lower town is quite the reverse, being built on the edge of the river with narrow streets and very dirty. The houses of the upper town have a peculiar bright glaring appearance at a distance, the roofs being covered with tin. There is a dryness in the air here as shown by the roofs of the houses in the country, which are of wood, and also the wooden fencing. You never see the green moss on outdoors woodwork such as we have in England.

May 18: Rainy day. Left Quebec at 7 A.M. for Boston, two days journey. Arrived at Richmond at 12 where I had to remain seven hours waiting for the train from Montreal. Spent the time as well as I could being quite alone, as I was the only passenger going that way. The reason of the delay is the summer trains between Portland and Montreal do not commence running till June.

Went over to a small Canadian village on the opposite side of the water. It is a fine high stony country about here, well suited for barley, but the people are poor. The railway runs through the village street but that has ceased to be a novelty with me. I was very glad when 7 o'clock arrived to find myself once more in the train. We don't get further than Island Pond that night, where we *lay over,* as the Yankees say. Here are two hotels where you would suppose one could not thrive, not unlike the Highlands of Scotland, a poor barren country studded with pines of no large growth.

The house at which I staid was very comfortable, good beds and clean, but in the morning it is so strange to an Englishman, but if he has not left some of his John Bull prejudices behind him by the time he arrives here, it is time he did, as his ideas of exclusiveness will not go down here.

You must all breakfast together at one table and at one time. I don't suppose they would provide a separate breakfast for anyone, even if he were a live lord.

This is about the American frontier and all, even to our baggage, is examined before starting, but they give you no trouble on that score.

May 19: Rainy day again. Cars leave at 7 so we have not had much time for sleep, having arrived at Island Pond at 12, but I have been too long travelling to ever refuse going to bed on a long journey when you have a chance, if the time is ever so short. It is far less fatigue the following day than constant travelling. We are now in the State of Maine. There is no mistaking Yankee land, where spitting, chewing and all other filthy habits are rampant in the railway cars and elsewhere. It seems rather extraordinary, but the moment you cross the frontier you can't but notice the marked difference in the habits of the people. On the Canadian lines of railway, as in England, the conductor is a clean orderly man ready and willing to give you every information. In the States, on the contrary, where John is always as good as his master and has great pleasure in asserting his position, the conductor looks upon it as quite a favour to tell you anything about the line, the arrival or departure of the trains, etc.; in fact, till you get used to their ways you have some difficulty in finding him out, as he is generally some swell of a fellow, you would never take him to be the conductor of the train. They seldom wear any distinctive badge. I was once, while in the West, asked for the omnibus fare by a man I certainly took to be one of the passengers and a very swell fellow too.

The northern part of the State of Maine between Island Pond and Portland, through which the line of railway runs, is very similar to what we passed through yesterday—poor and mountainous, not unlike Scotch scenery but wanting in heather, in the place of which it is studded with pines of small growth.

Arrived at Portland at 2 P.M., where we change cars and stay to dine. Here the Maine liquor law is in force in this free and enlightened State. You can't get a glass of beer or spirits for love or money. I believe they have some slang word, which I don't remember just now, but to sell brandy is contrary to law. Therefore, unless you know the password, you must wait till you get into the adjoining State. It so happened with me that I had not occasion to ask for any having always brandy with me, but it is a wonderful inconvenience to those who have occasion to call for it and are not aware of the law. Having staid a day longer in Quebec, through the kindness of my friends there, than I had intended, it limited my time in Portland, for which I was not sorry when I saw the place, as the railway runs the entire length of the town which gives a stranger a good idea of the port beyond, which there is nothing to see. I had expected seeing a much larger town as it is the port from which all the Canadian packets embark in the winter months while the St. Lawrence is blocked up with ice, and it is also the terminus of the Grand Trunk Railway of

Canada, the Company leasing that portion between this place and Island Pond.

Barnum is a very common name in America, the Smith of England. One of this name kept the refreshment room at Portland. The accommodation is very inferior, even at rooms such as these, to what you meet with at a similar junction in England. Arrived at Boston at 8 P.M., after a thirteen hours' run from Island Pond and two days from Quebec. There baggage arrangements are very superior. After you put your baggage in charge of the baggage master denoting your destination and taking a check for it, you never trouble yourself further till the end of your journey, when on presenting that check the baggage will be given you. On my arrival at Boston I did so, but one of my things could not be found. There are two lines from Portland to Boston and it appeared that it had been placed upon the wrong line, but the number on my check was sufficient security for its appearance, as it was soon brought to my hotel.

May 20: Rainy day again. Boston-Revere House—very good. Up early and received letters and newspapers from home, also three letters of introduction from Mr. T. Garfit to friends of his here which I found most valuable. Called first upon Col. Lawrence, 97 Beacon St., son of the late American Minister in England. Found him a most gentlemanly man. He very politely offered to show me the principal objects of the town and hoped I would dine with him and Mrs. Lawrence at 6 o'clock. As I had other letters and only one day to spend in Boston, we arranged to meet at

12 at the Revere House. Called upon The Hon. J. P. Bigelow, 95 Boylston and 4 Post Office Avenue (his place of business), a keen shrewd Yankee who entered most fully into my arrangements and was vastly pleased with the short account I gave him of my travels. He expressed himself quite sorry I had given so little time for Boston as he wished me to stay at his house.

On my arrival at the hotel in the evening from Col. Lawrence's I found a very kind note from him (Mr. Bigelow) expressing his regret at the shortness of my stay and hoped I would accept a present of books, among which was a short history of Boston, as a slight reminiscence of our acquaintance. He had visited Boston in England at the opening of the Church and was so pleased with the garden cultivation, as he calls it, of our English farms. I don't speak this from personal experience as my stay in Boston was so limited, but Col. Lawrence, who has seen most of the large cities in Europe and lived a considerable time in England, told me that the cultivation of lands within an area of ten miles of Boston, Mass., was very superior to anything he had seen in the neighbourhood of large cities in Europe.

Called upon The Hon. Mr. Story, formerly President of the Council of the Corporation of Boston, Mass. From home, left my card and heard no more of or from him. Col. Lawrence met me at 12 and took me to call upon the Mayor, who, finding I came from the neighbourhood of Boston in England, gave me a book (the Municipal Register) to take as a present from himself to the Mayor of Boston, England (Joseph Wren, Esq.). Went up the Bunker's Hill monument, from the top of which you have a fine panoramic view of the city. This Bunker's Hill is a spot of wonderful veneration among the Americans. In the lower part of the entrance hall are statues of eminent men (Americans of course) who figured on that occasion better known to them than us as the Battle of Bunker's Hill and is looked upon by the Yankees as the time when they "thrashed the Britishers," although I believe history makes us victorious on that particular occasion.

Be that as it may, American independence resulted from it and I must confess that my sympathies are more with the men who fought for throwing off the British yoke on that occasion than with those who resisted it, which I think the subsequent progress of the people has fully justified.

Col. Lawrence, while showing me one of these statues, said, "I had some English gentleman here the other day as you may be, and one of them asked on looking at that statue (Warren) 'And who was Warren?' I was quite struck with his ignorance."

I, like my ignorant countryman, did not know who Warren was but of course kept my counsel and Col. L never knew, but the fact is American history does not extend far back as even Boston, which was among the earliest settlements, was an untracked wilderness two hundred and fifty years back, known only to the Red Indians, so you always find Yankees commence with the declaration of independence when they threw off the British yoke—consequently every man, woman and child in the country learn from their infancy every detail in connection therewith, which they have ready to instil into a stranger on every occasion. It would have been well if they had retained the manners as well as the language of the Anglo-Saxon race.

Boston is an exceedingly well-built town, chiefly of red brick. It has quite an air of wealth about it, which you can't mistake. The streets are on the irregular English plan, very different from the general American system. There is a public park, Beacon St., where Col. Lawrence resides, forming one side. One of the buildings forming the opposite side of the square is the public library, founded by many wealthy contributors. Among the chief is Mr. Bates of the firm Baring & Co., London, who contributed $50,000 towards the erection of the building in addition to a like amount for books which are free to every resident in the town of Boston to take home for a limited time (a fortnight). It is the finest democracy possible, as many of the most wealthy in the place equally avail themselves of it (if they have not the works in their own libraries) with the poor man, and to show how admirably the system works the librarian tells me they never lose any books—in fact the annual loss of books is so trifling that it is of no moment. It speaks great things in a distribution of 200,000 vol. annually, as it has not been established more than seven years. I saw the History of Boston, Lincolnshire (by Pishey Thompson) presented by the Mayor and Aldermen of Boston, England, to the Citizens of Boston, Massachusetts, in which among other names I noticed those of Fred Cooke, Mayor, Sharp, Lewin, Caistor, Lewin Jnr. Tho' Wright, Fucker, T. Collis, etc., Calthrop, Town Clerk. After a very pleasant day I dined with Col. Lawrence, 97 Beacon St., and found him a most agreeable gentlemanly man, having moved in the first society in England. Greatly surprised to find that he and his friend, who dined with us, drew so favourable a comparison of our form of Government against their own, and even more so to find both Mrs. Lawrence and her husband express their sympathy with the Southerners on the slave question, a subject I should have never dreamt of mentioning in Boston, which I had always considered to be the very hotbed of abolitionism.

How much conversation about England. I only wonder that people holding these views prefer living in America. Sorry to part with such nice people in this country, but my time was limited, having to leave early the following morning as I was anxious to arrive in New York on Saturday night if possible.

May 21: I had intended going down to Albany by the Hudson and thence to New York but Mr. Lawrence told me the most beautiful part of the scenery of the Hudson was between New York and West Point. So I left Boston by rail to N.Y. at 8 o'clock, where we arrived at 4 P.M. in a pelting rain. It has rained the whole of this week since it commenced on Tuesday morning in Quebec. The country between Boston and New York looks older and better-built than any part I have seen of the United States. You never see the stumps of trees on the land here and more ground is in grass.

New York station: This is a babel but I knew their ways too well, having been here before, so I immediately made for the St. Nicholas stage coach, which I have described elsewhere, gave my baggage ticket to the driver and in due time was landed at the hotel. It seemed quite like home to me to be driving up Broadway after my long wanderings, it being past seven weeks this day since I left the hotel, having travelled over more than five thousand miles of country and been in all the variations of climate between Ther. at 123 and ice and snow on the ground above Quebec.

Although the advantages are decidedly in favour of a man travelling alone, only those who have taken long journeys by themselves can appreciate the satisfaction there is in getting again among friends. Did not get so nice a bedroom as on my first visit, which they offered to change after the first night, but you soon get used to anything so I let things keep as they were. Glad to get back to the comforts of a large hotel. Went immediately to the Post Office for letters. Found two, and nine newspapers, which last I should have declined taking, having seen most of the news at the clubs, but I must either take all or none. Very sorry to hear of Mr. Burrell's death, which appears to have been much accelerated by his own imprudence. Much electioneering news which I had previously seen at the club rooms where my friends had been good enough to introduce me.

May 22: Sunday. Rainy day again, making six consecutive rainy days. Staid in the hotel most of the day as I was not well after my journey. The first man I met I knew in the St. Nicholas was Old Bidden, waiting like myself to return in the *Persia* on Wednesday. Glad to meet him as he came out with me. Called in the afternoon upon Capt. Judkins at the Everett House. Found the *Persia* very full for Wednesday, every berth taken and many turned away. I agreed, at his recommendation, to dispose of my spare berth (having taken the whole cabin to myself in March, paying $65 in addition for so doing) to Chevalier Nychoff, as he reported him, although an American, to be a man of clean habits, shaving and washing once a day and not one of those chewing, spitting, disgusting Yankees, of whom I had such a horror of putting up with for ten days in the same berth, that I paid the additional half fare to have the berth to myself.

He paid to me through Judkins $65 and would pay the company a like sum and was very glad of the opportunity. It was important to him to get to Europe as he was on his way to China on Government business. I afterwards had no reason to regret it as I found him a very agreeable fellow, which was even pleasanter than having the room to myself, particularly as we had, although a large number of passengers, few whose acquaintance I cared to make.

Judkins and I got into a row with a cabman at the Everett House, who wanted $1½ (6/3d English) for taking us to the St. Nicholas, not more than half a mile. The fellow was very abusive when we told him we could not spend our money in that way, but what vexed him more was we took the rail at five cents (Englishman like) rather than be done by cabby. We then had to walk on leaving the car, I think further than if we had walked the whole way, raining hard all the while, but they are such an extortionate set of thieves here, worse than any place I ever met with. The omnibus travelling in New York is good and cheap, if you happen to be on the line of either the street omnibuses or the cars.

May 23: Spent the day up the Hudson River as I knew there would be no satisfying a Yankee if I told him I had seen all America but had not been up the North River to West Point. (Say all this through your nose.) If they knew you had not seen it they would swear by all that was holy that there was no scenery in the world equal to it, so I made up my mind to get up early and see what it was as far as West Point, which I ascertained comprised the best of it, and left the hotel early, half past 6, to catch the first boat up the river to Albany. The scenery is very picturesque and the banks are pleasantly studded with villas for many miles. Saw the *Persia* on the New Jersey side of the river ready for Wednesday. They always make her up very smart and clean before leaving port. It would be a very pleasant day's excursion up the Hudson if they had a band of music on board instead of that confounded hurdi-gurdi driven by steam—a pure Yankee notion, anything to save labour in this country. They drive the bellows of an old crazy organ by the spare steam which saves a boy, consequently the old thing is never out of wind. They then engage one of those Grundu boys, who all know music, as a general help on board. Whenever he has any spare time or we approach a landing place he is sure to be firing away at full speed and as the old thing has but three tunes it is rather monotonous. How the bus drivers do swear they can't get a horse near the landing when those things are at work.

The scenery of the river becomes more bold as you approach West Point. This is the great national Military Educational Establishment, where the American youth are instructed in the art of war. There is a very good hotel here standing on a pleasing eminence on a bend of the river commanding a view of the river each way. Staid to lunch and then crossed the river to catch the Albany train to New York, where we arrived in about two hours. The line is constructed at the foot of the rocks at the edge of the river, consequently consists of many curves, but I think it is the fastest-running line I have travelled upon in the United States.

May 24: New York. Up early as I had much to do. Went first to Smith & Co., Beekman St. to buy a print of Chicago, which to my disappointment could not be obtained in New York, but most fortunate in finding there a number of very valuable prints on sale far better than any I saw in the shops in Broadway. Purchased there views of Boston, St. Louis, Falls of St. Anthony, Montreal, Charleston, S.C., Havana, also to 366 Broadway for Philadelphia, New York, Falls of Niagara. Thence to Williams & Stevens, 353 Broadway, for prints from Church's great picture of the Falls of Niagara. The original painting, which has been on view in New Orleans, had just come in and they were good enough to allow me to see it.

The purchaser of a proof has two chances and the print one chance for the original, whenever it is drawn for, which I understand will be the way of disposing of it when they have got the requisite number of subscribers. Therefore, I stand for three chances whenever that event takes place, although I look upon it as rather remote.

Called upon my friend, Mr. Brown, 45 South St., through whose kindness I had received such valuable introductions in the South, to thank him and to give him my views on the slavery question, in which he takes so much interest. I was very sorry my time was up that I could not spend a day with him. He introduced me to his son-in-law, Col. Smith, who is a large planter in Texas and holds many slaves. He told me he had no doubt he should raise eleven bales of cotton to the field hand this year.

Called also upon Messrs. Catlin & Switt, 31 Chambers St., to thank them in like manner, also on Messrs. Elliott & Co. who gave me a letter to Mr. Stone in Guelph. Very busy the whole day as I had so much to do before leaving the following morning and did not get in till late. Purchased two buffalo robes by the advice of a gentleman from Montreal (which is the great emporium for them) as he was going to get two for me direct from the Ottawa and send them to England, but thinks these quite equal to what he could get there. Went to Duncan & Sherman, Bankers, and obtained a draft on London for the balance of my account with them. Packing up. How the weather had changed since I left New York! Then it was very cold, all the drivers wearing buffalo skins, etc. Now it is quite hot enough to be pleasant. I am well satisfied I selected the proper time for visiting the United States. Perhaps had I been a month earlier I might have gone further South and visited Cuba and New Orleans, and a fortnight later in Canada would have been pleasanter inasmuch as this country would have been seen to greater advantage, but on the whole, considering the vast extent of country I have seen, I consider myself to have been very fortunate.

May 25: Up early and left the hotel with Bidden and his friend at 8 o'clock to New Jersey, to take the first boat to the *Persia*. Both of us having had some experience in travelling, we know well the rush there would be on the third and fourth boats to get down, and as to getting your own things into your berth, it would be out of the question that day unless you came by the early boats. Got down very quietly and everything to our berths before many passengers began to arrive. Although all your baggage is on board, if you don't mind, some of it will get stowed away in the hold which you never see again till you land, which was the case with an unfortunate packing case of mine too large for any berth. It gave me more trouble at Liverpool than all the rest of my baggage.

I can't say how many people came on board the *Persia*

that morning, passengers and their friends coming to see them off, as it was a most beautiful day, but the deck—large as it is—was quite full. At last, about 11 o'clock, they began gradually to return, till the mail boat took off all who did not intend setting sail for England. I counted fifty-three sacks of letters come on board.

There are often some very amusing scenes on board to anyone studying character, particularly if he is an old traveller and takes things gently.

I was much amused with one woman (American lady) who displayed a monstrous amount of jewellery about her person and whose husband was dressed in the very height of vulgarity, and the little boy who I always called a "Yankee institution to himself," having such a peculiar dress and boots, all bound for Europe, no doubt for the first time. When cabby brought the last piece of luggage on board the lady said to her nearest neighbour loud enough for everyone to hear, "Goodbye, Russell. Ah, poor fellow, our coachman feels our going away very much." I should think from appearances, if the truth were known, that man Russell was a common hack cab driver in New York hand and glove with them at home.

I often thought of poor Russell when I used to see my lady come down to breakfast in the saloon, decked out in her jewels and lace. No doubt her husband kept a store of some sort in New York, perhaps a fish store for aught I know.

At 1.15 P.M. we fired two guns and off. Waving of handkerchiefs among friends as the great ship and the tug boat part company, together with the evident grief among many of the passengers, cause rather a gloom on leaving port, which those who have ever left land for any length of time know well. For my own part I was glad to be once more on board the *Persia*, hoping for a prosperous voyage and safe return to the old country. I thought the harbour of New York looked very beautiful as we left, the trees being now in full foliage on the banks.

The ground is so peculiarly well chosen for a large city, being on the point of land formed by the confluence of two large rivers, the East River and the Hudson, with, I should think, as fine a bay as any on the Atlantic. If anything will make an Englishman proud of his own country, it is visiting this. Although speaking our language they have no feeling in common with us and I don't know any people professing friendship who would sooner see England humbled than the Americans.

What are they but a compound of Germans, Scotch, Dutch, Irish?—in fact every nation under heaven is represented in New York. They have but little of the true Anglo-Saxon blood among them. At the same time, I am happy to say, there are many honourable exceptions, of which I have reason to speak highly and I can't conclude these remarks without acknowledging the marked kindness and courtesy I met with on all occasions—the more so as I knew hardly three people in the country previous to my visit. Yet through introductions I took out with me and acquaintances

I formed during my travels, I visited but few places of importance but where I met with friends. Many of my friends since my return have observed how much you have seen in the time. I can only say travelling is like many other things, quite a matter of business—that is, if you wish to see all you can within a given period; and in a journey of this magnitude, unless you lay out a plan before you start and keep to it, it will only end in vexation that your time is gone and that by staying a day longer here and another there, that at last you are so pushed for time that you hurry over places you afterwards regret.

Plan of journey before leaving and where I expected letters

Proposed time		Actual Arrival and Stay
April 7th	Washington	April 5th—7th
14th—22nd	Charleston and the South	9th—14th
April 29th	Through the cotton country and up to St. Louis	28th
May 3rd	Chicago	May 1st
7th & 8th	Niagara Falls	6th—7th
10th	Toronto	7th and 8th
14th	Montreal	13th and 14th
16th	Quebec	15th—17th
21st	Boston	20th
23rd	New York	21st

When at Boston, Mass., I showed this to an old gentleman there, Mr. Bigelow. I thought he would have never ceased talking about, he was so pleased with the correctness with which I had kept my time. There is but little to describe on board ship in a ten days' voyage. Our homeward trip was not nearly so pleasant as our outward one, although the weather was rougher going out. We had 235 passengers coming home, many of them Americans, and not nearly such nice people as those going out. On 28th, 3 P.M., ship in sight full sail. She had not the civility to hoist her colours in answer to ours, so we set her down for a Yankee, a regular down-Easter near the sun rising, showing such a breach of good manners.

On the ninth day the Irishmen on board began to talk of smelling the peat fires of old Ireland, and true to their reckoning we saw the Irish coast at 10 A.M. Some declared they saw it the night before. I can't say that I did although we all strained our eyes to see it if possible.

At 6 P.M. on that evening (exactly nine days from leaving New York allowing for the difference in time running East) we passed Holyhead. It was a pretty rough sea for the Irish steamers coming in from Kingston, but our great ship seemed to ride so majestically on the waves that we never felt it, particularly after being used to the motion for ten days. What a glorious sight it is to see land again, particularly your native shore. The pilot was on board an hour from Holyhead, who brought us newspapers which were highly prized as we had not received any English news for near three weeks, having just missed the *Asia* going into New York, and our own time ten days made us very anxious. It is quite a comedy to study character on such an occasion, to watch where every man's particular interest lay. One man wants to know how the war is progressing, another the price of cotton, another the price of Consols, etc., etc. We got the latest paper and Everitt, who was a very forward fussy fellow, was requested to read it. One little incident amused some of us very much. Among other news, Everitt was reading the arrival of the American packets which no one cared to know about. Just at that time old Judkins came in and hearing when the *Niagara* got in he hollered out in his gruff voice, "When did she get in, read that again," showing where his thoughts were.

Night came on and we knew but little of going up the river. At daybreak we found ourselves alongside Birkenhead on a rainy morning, so characteristic of our English climate. I must confess I was rather vexed it did rain that particular morning for I heard many Americans who had been over before remark to some of their countrymen who had not, that it was customary for it to rain in this climate every other day. Custom House officers on board to examine luggage. They are only strict with tobacco and books. 9/6d per lb. you pay on tobacco, the same on that as cigars. They only allow you to pay duty on 5 lbs. of cigars. If you have a larger number they won't allow you to land them unless you import ten thousand. I had more than the quantity allowed, so charged half of them in the name of the Chevalier on which I paid the duty. I should have got off well with him with my baggage but for one unfortunate case of

American views which they had stowed away in the hold. It took so long to find that I was detained as long as anyone, so he had very kindly offered to land me when he did. (Anyone connected with Government as he was and having dispatches on board has the privilege of being landed before the other passengers if he wishes.) It was a drenching rain that morning, notwithstanding which (thanks to Capt. Judkins) every passenger, 235 in number, had got their baggage examined, and himself and passengers left the ship in two hours. Bid adieu to the *Persia,* Capt. Judkins and the officers, having carried me safely twice over the Atlantic. Arrived at the Adelphi Hotel; very jolly to breakfast on English soil again. Found it just possible to save the Hull train and get home that night, so left my breakfast upon the table as there was only just time to get a cab and drive to the Exchange Station.

Arrived safely at Firsby Station 9.18 after an absence of nearly twelve weeks. It is only those who have travelled that can appreciate the pleasure and satisfaction there is in once more setting foot upon English soil after a lengthened absence. Not only a meeting with relatives and friends but in looking back and recounting the various incidents of travel through an extended tour. Although I left home much to the surprise and contrary to the advice and wishes of many of my best friends, I shall never regret the step I then took.

In a journey of upwards of eleven thousand miles from the city of Quebec in the North to the cotton and rice fields of South Carolina, Georgia and Alabama in the South, thence to the prairies of the West, beyond the Mississippi, embracing every variety of soil and climate from the cold of Canada to an almost tropical sun. There is an immense deal to see and much to learn, and I would recommend any young man having the means and the time at his disposal before settling in this country to see America and judge for himself.

There are so many things to interest an Englishman— the rapid rise of cities, particularly in the West; take for instance Chicago, now numbering more than 100,000 people, which thirty years ago was merely an Indian trading post. It is now the centre of more miles of railway than even London itself and can show stores and buildings which would be no disgrace to that great city. Chicago is no solitary instance. St. Louis and many others are equally so. The timber trade of Canada or the cotton productions of the Southern States are either of them on a scale which many Englishmen have but a slight idea of.

As a people I do not admire them. They are such a conceited, self-sufficient, rough lot, with the greatest love for their own country I ever met with, even more so than the Scotch. They claim to have the highest mountains, longest rivers, fastest steamboats, etc., in the known world. Even the Falls of Niagara I don't think they consider to be on British territory. Get into conversation with a Yankee about the beauties of Niagara, he is sure to say, "Mighty fine water power, I guess you have nothing like that in your country." They are such a contemptible, money-grabbing lot; even that mighty fine water power, as they call it, they would like to turn to some purpose of trade. On the American side now it is studded with mills, etc.

At the same time that self-reliance and go-aheadness has been the great secret of their unparalleled success as a people. In building cities I consider they are far before us, as they are laid out and built on a system conducive to good drainage and ventilation. They are wanting in good roads. The Canadians, like the English, make the roads good first. The Yankee, on the other hand, builds the city, leaving the roads to another generation.

In hotels they are far before us. I only wish the English would take a leaf out of their book in hotel-keeping. We have nothing in Europe on the magnificent scale, combining the comfort and charges you find in the first-class American hotels. I take it the people being of that restless, active turn are always travelling, consequently the hotels are generally full, which enables them to keep a larger staff, and there not being that great distinction of class we have in an old country materially assists in conducting these monster hotels on a uniform scale.

I think there is much to be admired in their forms of religion having no state church. Every denomination is on an equal footing; the result of which is that every man feels sufficient interest in the creed he professes to support, which produces a greater attachment between the Minister and his people than in the Established Church in England, where a man is quite regardless of the feelings of his flock. Such a system could not be tolerated on the Continent of America, as has recently been proved in Canada by the withdrawal of the Canadian reserves.

The accompanying statement shows the predominant religious parties in the United States, taken from the census of 1850:

RELIGIOUS DENOMINATIONS—CENSUS 1850

	No. of Churches	Aggregate Accommodation	Average Accommodation	Total value of Church property	Value
Methodist	12,467	4,209,333	337	$14,636,671	$1,174
Baptist	8,791	3,130,878	356	10,931,382	1,244
Presbyterian	4,584	2,040,316	445	14,369,889	3,135
Congregational	1,674	795,177	475	7,973,962	4,763
Episcopal	1,422	625,213	440	11,261,970	7,919
Roman Catholic	1,112	620,950	558	8,973,838	8,069
Unitarian	243	137,367	565	3,268,122	13,449
Jewish	31	16,575	534	371,600	1,987

with many others too numerous to mention.

It appears the Methodists take the lead in numbers and also in the values of Church property. The Baptists rank second in numbers although the Presbyterians have a larger amount of Church property. I have not seen any statement giving the actual numbers in each state but my own observations would lead me to suppose that the Presbyterians are a more numerous body in the Southern States than in the Northern.

If any man has a doubt as to the propriety of voting by

ballot, let him come out here and see how the system works in the great republic, where the sovereign will of the people rules everything. Every office is elective from the President downwards, even the Judges of this land are voted into office by men on whom they may have to sit in judgment on a future day. I should think even Cobden himself, if he would express all he thinks, is not so charmed with the system, having seen the working of it in America, as he would wish us to believe. It appears to me the Government of the country is carried on not unlike what our Municipal Corporations in England have come to. The most unscrupulous, pushing men get into offices which those better qualified by their intelligence and education stand aloof from, not willing to enter into competition with such. Whenever they change their President, which they do every four years, it is a general move all throughout the States. Every man, let his office be ever so unimportant, changes when a new President is elected, consequently it has the effect of making every man a politician, as there is not a township in the Union but what is affected by the change.

Slavery is a question puzzling wiser heads than mine, although every Englishman, particularly if he has never been from home, thinks himself quite competent to give an opinion upon it. I can't talk to Englishmen about it, as those not having seen it can form but an incorrect opinion on the subject. I only wish more of my countrymen could see slavery as it is in the Southern States of America and judge fairly, between one man and another, whether all the onus rests with the Southern planter who grows the cotton. Let him ask himself whether he entirely frees the British manufacturer who makes up the raw material and whether we, on this side of the Atlantic, are not tending to tighten the bonds of slavery quite as much as the Southerner who grows the cotton. What has caused the value of negroes to rise cent per cent but the increased value of their productions, and can any intelligent man travel through our manufacturing districts of Lancashire and the West Riding of Yorkshire without asking himself the question what has caused these towns to rise so rapidly but the manufacture of American *slave grown* cotton? I don't wish for a moment to advocate the extension of slavery but merely speak of what I have seen with my own eyes. Not like an English philanthropist, they tell a tale of who proposed going down South to judge for himself. He got no further than Philadelphia on his way, which he took for a slave state as he was waited upon by blacks, and finding something in his soup he could not make out he left the place in disgust vowing he could not live among such cannibals as he had got so far South where they boiled down the young niggers into soup.

I met a man coming home in the *Persia* who had been out for a like purpose—I don't mean to eat soup but to see slavery. I found he had not been further South than Maryland; he was condemning slavery right and left. I asked him, "Have you seen plantation life where the cotton is grown?" He said he had not. I told him on no account tell your friends in England that you have seen slavery, as I consider you have seen only the worst features of the system. The climate of Maryland does not require slave labour in the cultivation of the soil, consequently the natural increase of the slave population in that state are reared like so many young calves and sent down to the Southern markets for sale.

We all acknowledge the evil of slavery. I have myself witnessed scenes in the slave markets of the South and West that would make an Englishman shudder; but it has grown so gigantic that it is a most difficult question to deal with. The people who own these slaves did not import them, as the majority of them have been bred and raised on the plantations where they live.

In the Southern States in a climate where cotton can't be produced by white labour you find out of a population of ten million more than three and a half million in slavery. What can you do with them? As to setting them free, it is monstrous to talk of such a thing. They are neither prepared for it nor would their condition be improved by it. There is not that self-reliance in the negro character you see in the white man. I think the fact of the large numbers speaks much in favour of the Planter, for if these people were in the oppressed, ill-used state most Englishmen think they are, they could rise and murder every white man upon the plantation, which the blacks would outnumber twenty to one, but far from that being the case, I have reason to believe that where they are fairly treated they are *devotedly attached to the Planters and their families.*

I would recommend those Exeter Hall philanthropists and many well-meaning people in England who rail so strongly against slavery, to extend their operations in reclaiming the "Poor African" among his native tribes, rather than interfere with the slave holders of the South, whose people (on a well regulated estate) are better clothed, housed, fed and generally cared for than half the labouring poor in many counties in England and have advantages of religious instruction which they never possessed in their native tribes, and I may say with truth, the observance of the Sabbath by the negro population in the Southern cities would shame a white population in many of our villages and towns in England.

I think I have made it my study to see all classes of society, from the wealthy Southern Planter to the squatter in the West. I may have come to wrong conclusions but I hope I have not taken a prejudiced view of things, but I must say the class of people who most disappointed me (for I did not expect to like the Yankee with his tobacco-chewing propensities and the accompaniments) was the British settler in the West. It is a government requirement before a man becomes an American citizen and can exercise his vote, for which he has five years allowed, that he should renounce allegiance to every government but that of the United States, which they appear to do most effectually in spirit as well as in the letter. They seem to have lost all feeling for the country of their birth, in fact I should say from conversation with many of them, they have rather an antipathy to the old country than otherwise. Whether it is that their tempers are soured by the country not being what they expected or that having spent their money and consequently have no probability of ever returning, I can't say, but such struck me as being the case.